THE

THE WITCH'S BOOK
— OF —
LOVE

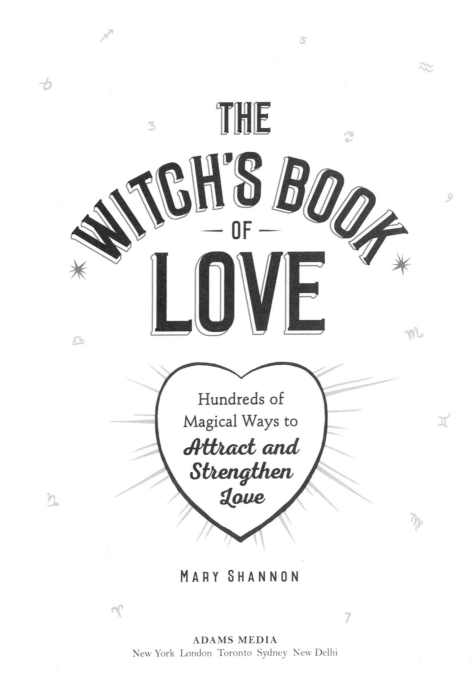

THE WITCH'S BOOK OF LOVE

Hundreds of Magical Ways to *Attract and Strengthen Love*

MARY SHANNON

ADAMS MEDIA
New York London Toronto Sydney New Delhi

Aadamsmedia

Adams Media
An Imprint of Simon & Schuster, Inc.
57 Littlefield Street
Avon, Massachusetts 02322

First Adams Media hardcover edition
January 2020

ADAMS MEDIA and colophon are
trademarks of Simon & Schuster.

For information about special discounts for
bulk purchases, please contact Simon &
Schuster Special Sales at 1-866-506-1949 or
business@simonandschuster.com.

The Simon & Schuster Speakers Bureau can
bring authors to your live event. For more
information or to book an event contact
the Simon & Schuster Speakers Bureau at
1-866-248-3049 or visit our website at
www.simonspeakers.com.

Interior design and illustrations by
Priscilla Yuen

Manufactured in the United States
of America

10 9 8 7 6 5 4 3 2 1

Library of Congress Cataloging-in-
Publication Data has been applied for.

ISBN 978-1-5072-1262-2
ISBN 978-1-5072-1263-9 (ebook)

Contains material adapted from the
following titles published by Adams Media,
an Imprint of Simon & Schuster, Inc.: *Love
Craft*, edited by Anna Haywood, copyright
© 2013, ISBN 978-1-4405-6066-8 and *The
Secret Power of You* by Meera Lester,
copyright © 2012, ISBN 978-1-4405-4013-4.

CONTENTS

CHAPTER 4

SPELLS:
Enchant Your Way *Into* Your Partner's Heart · 175

CHAPTER 5

MAGICAL LOVE
Is Here to Stay · 241

INTRODUCTION

Wondering if that special someone could be a true love connection? Want to match up with someone who shares your passion and interests? Looking to attract a partner for life? Let the infinite powers of the universe lend you a hand!

The Witch's Book of Love has all the spells and solutions to help you on your quest for love. You'll discover how to use numerology, palmistry, astrology, and spellcraft to meet someone special, strengthen a current relationship, or find your forever love match. The tools in this book will help you learn more about yourself and the special people in your life so you can get on the path to true love:

✦ Numerology shows you how to look at the numbers that make up the core of who you are and what makes you tick. Are you an introvert or an extrovert? Do you want to travel the world, or are you happier in your own backyard? Are your partner's key numbers a good match for yours?

+ Palmistry opens your eyes to your unique talents and tendencies and reveals what's in store for you in the future. And, once you've read your own palm, you can read your partner's and enjoy both the intimate touch and the information you learn!

+ Astrology is a powerful way to see how well your personality will match with other people's. Knowing more about your astrological sign (and your potential partner's) can tell you if you two might be a match made in the heavens—or if you're better staying light-years apart.

+ Spells that you can customize for your particular situation will help you connect with the special someone you're meant to be with. Create a sacred space in your home to conduct these easy but powerful spells, find a god or goddess to call upon, and send your call for a partner out into the universe.

This book will give you a better understanding of who you are and what you want in a relationship so you can go out and find it. With this complete guide to magical matchmaking, you'll be in the relationship of your dreams in no time. Stop waiting for the right person to show up on your doorstep—make it happen yourself!

Chapter 1

NUMEROLOGY:

THE MAGIC OF LOVE BY THE NUMBERS

Many people think of numbers the way accountants, mathematicians, and scientists think of them—as inanimate figures used to calculate or manipulate quantities of things. But there's another way to look at numbers too—as digits that are alive, imbued with energy, and animated by a life force. The ancient Egyptians believed in this immense power of numbers, and also gave numbers active and receptive and male and female characteristics.

Although ideas about the mystical aspects of numbers permeated the ancient world, the Greek mathematician Pythagoras was likely the first to organize and popularize those esoteric ideas into what would become the art of numerology. Numerology can be used for a range of things—to help understand yourself at a deeper level, to help you find the right date for an event, or to better understand a love interest's personality. Once you know how to access the power inherent in numerology, you will be able to enhance your own life, making it richer, happier, and full of love.

WHAT IS NUMEROLOGY?

Numerology is the metaphysical study of numbers and their potential significance in terms of your life or future. The most important numbers in your life, according to numerology, aren't your bank account balances or salary but rather your birth name and birthdate. From those numbers, you discover your purpose in life, your special qualities, and your life lessons—in short, information that will empower you to have the life (and love) meant just for you.

Witches believe that each number has a profound role to play in the universe and that the placement or alteration of the numbers could effect change and influence outcomes in a person's life. Numbers can help guide you and illuminate the path you want in questions big and small related to goals, decision-making, love, and so on. As you strive to live a full and rich love life, let the language of numerology's numbers and symbols lead the way.

✦ *Magical Musings* ✦

Your intuition plays a vital role as you work with any magical tool, be it numerology, palmistry, astrology, or spellcasting. True intuition is your deep inner conviction that something is correct. Although what you intuit may seem illogical and not provable using facts, reason, or logic, the insight can nonetheless guide you, especially at the turning points of your life. Give your intuition free rein as you now begin to explore these tools of witchcraft and how they relate to your love life.

Mathematics versus Numerology

Numbers can be used in two basic ways: physical mathematics and metaphysical numerology. Mathematics and numerology both rely on the use of numbers to produce information or to manipulate the environment, but they are different:

+ Mathematics is employed in the construction of conceptual systems for understanding Earth's physical laws.

+ Numerology expresses metaphysical insights about numbers as they pertain to your life and the mysteries of the universe.

The Connection Between Energy and Numbers

Everything in the universe is made up of some form of energy. This energy vibrates, and the vibration has a frequency. The frequency at which an object vibrates helps connect the object to certain characteristics, energy values, qualities, and the like.

—— ✦ *Magical Musings* ✦ ——

Think of how many numbers you run into throughout your day. Witches find meaning in such mundane moments and will use these numbers to enhance the energy around them. If you microwave your meal for 2 minutes and 22 seconds, what influence do all those 2s (and the 6 that they add up to) have on the food you are about to eat?

The same is true for your numbers. The numbers that describe you (your birthdate, for example) have a symbolic meaning and an energy value that numerologists use to describe you—your personality, strengths and weaknesses, life purpose, relationships, talents and abilities, and more.

— ✦ *Magical Musings* ✦ —

Nature and numbers are closely connected, especially in witchcraft. Counting the number of petals on a flower will quickly tell you the essential properties available for spells. For example, an eight-petaled flower is helpful for spells involving prosperity, while a five-petaled flower promotes change. The phases of the Moon, marked in twenty-eight-day cycles, is another important numerical figure in natural magic.

If you think about it, you probably already impart meaning or energy to certain numbers. Perhaps you've been a single person in a group of couples, or the only person in a dark parking lot at midnight. In those cases, one might be a lonely number. In groups, however, people say there is safety or strength "in numbers."

— ✦ *Magical Musings* ✦ —

The use of symbols is important to every witch. Symbols are used as a means of communicating with the divine and the universe. They are considered a universal language that spirits use when passing on messages from the other side.

The use of these symbols, so organic in nature, opened the way for nonverbal communication that encouraged intuition, inspiration, creativity, ingenuity, and imagination for more meaningful, happier lives for people. Gradually, as people developed the ability to move from symbols to numbers, each number took on a specific meaning, and numerology was born.

THE NUMBERS TO KNOW

The single-digit numbers, 1 through 9, are the backbone of numerology and provide key information. Numerologists also pay special attention to the master numbers—11, 22, and 33—which can either be reduced (by adding the single digits that make up the number, such as 1 + 1) or kept whole. In numerology, the numbers 1 through 9, 11, 22, and 33 are significant because of the energy values, symbolism, and meaning associated with those values. Numbers always carry the same vibrational frequency, and once you understand what that is, you can easily harness the value and energy of numbers.

THE NINE PURE NUMBERS

The numbers 1 through 9 are considered pure numbers. Each represents a pure quality, or in other words, a characteristic that is unaffected by any other quality. All the other numbers come from a combination of pure numbers. Just as red, blue, and yellow are the primary colors and all other colors are a combination of the primary ones, so are 1, 2, 3, 4, 5, 6, 7, 8, and 9 the primary numbers, with all other numbers being formed from them (through reduction by adding them together). Hence, the number 10, a compound number, may be expressed as $1 + 0 = 1$.

✦ Magical Musings ✦

The number 10 is different from the other compound numbers; it *contains* all the qualities of 1 through 9 and *becomes* all of them. The difference between a 10-derived 1 and a pure 1 is that a pure 1 is like a beautiful tree in your backyard, complete in itself, while a 10-derived 1 is like your backyard. The number 10 expands the singular in 1 as it absorbs all of life's experiences.

Ancient numerologists assigned the number 10 as Earth's vibe number. Everything on Earth, according to numerology, happens in groups of 10. Many ancient calendars had 10 months, which makes sense according to numerology.

MASTER NUMBERS

While most numbers are reduced down to the nine pure numbers, master numbers are certain numbers that are left as they are: 11, 22, and 33. These numbers are special in numerology and considered to have extra potential.

If you encounter a master number, take notice. Individuals with master numbers in their numerological charts have the capability to do great work and make an impact on the world, but in order to do this, they usually have to go through a trial or an experience that pushes their limits and allows them to break free from the common mold.

Master numbers have a duality in their vibration. They can be left as they are or reduced further to their pure state (2, 4, 6). This means that each has the essence of its higher self as well as its pure number and can manifest in both ways. If you have a master number as one of your core numbers, read both the master and the pure state and see which description fits you better. It could be that the higher form of the number will express itself more with age and experience.

The Number Zero

Zero is not a number that is traditionally used or looked at in numerology. It does, however, have a vibration all its own and a significance that you can see expressed in the world around you. If you encounter a zero, you will find that it has the energy of purity to it. Think of the moment when a race is about to start and a timer is set to zero; there is a feeling of possibility in that instant. Anything can happen in the time to come—you could win the race, you could fall and injure yourself, or you could finish last. This number also represents oneness and the power of the Source in all that is around you. Zero vibrates to universal love and contains an edge of innocence wherever it touches.

✦ *Magical Musings* ✦

In nature, certain shapes and symbols are common. Early humans noticed that, too, and began using symbols such as circles, semicircles, and triangles in their numerical language. Later, within the art of numerology, numbers and symbols became endowed with rich, esoteric meaning and energy value. For example, a circle is a line with no end and no beginning. The circle is a line of wholeness and completion, simultaneously flowing and completing. The circle in nature can be seen in fruits and berries, the midday Sun, and the Full Moon, and in mathematics the circle is a key part of geometry. Before doing magical work, many witches cast a circle. This distinguishes a space between the outside mundane energies and inner magical practices. In witchcraft, circles are both protective and a source of power.

YOUR CORE NUMBERS

Four numbers make up the basis for your numerological profile. To find these numbers, all you need to know is your birth name and birthdate. The vibration and frequency from these numbers come together to make up a profile of your personality.

Before trying to improve your love life, it is helpful to drill down into who *you* really are. You should discover what makes you tick—your hopes and dreams, your life purpose, and those special talents and abilities that you don't always recognize or appreciate. Looking at your core numbers will help you do this. They will help you know yourself and your desires in a more intimate way.

Once you learn about yourself, you can then use the birth name and birthdate of your partner to get to know them better as well. See if your interests in life mesh, or if, for example, you are a homebody and your romantic interest is an explorer. Numbers are important, but also don't discount that gut feeling you get when you are around the person. Listen to your intuition; it will never steer you wrong.

LIFE PATH NUMBER

The first and most important number to determine is your life path number, which tells what path you are heading down. This number can give you insight into some lessons or challenges that you may encounter along your journey. It is considered the most essential number in numerology and is found by adding the digits of your birthdate. These create the vibrational basis for the moment you were born and the foundation of the life you chose to lead.

To add insight into your life path, most numerologists also take a look at the actual day you were born. This date gives hints into any specific talents or purposes that you brought with you into this lifetime. By combining your life path number with your actual day of birth, you can see what areas in life you may excel at and where you may fall short.

For example, if you were born on October 12, 1992, you would first find your life path number by adding the digits in your full birthdate:

> **October:** 10 ... 1 + 0 = 1
> **12:** 1 + 2 = 3
> **1992:** 1 + 9 + 9 + 2 = 21 ... 2 + 1 = 3
> **Life path number:** 1 + 3 + 3 = 7

Your life path number would be a 7. In general, those with life path number 7 tend to be spiritual and find themselves drawn to learning about the great mysteries of life.

To further distinguish your life path characteristics from other individuals who resonate with the number 7, you would take the actual day of birth (12) and add the digits: 1 + 2 = 3. Those who vibrate with the number 3 tend to have a creative streak that allows them to combine two sources into something new and unique.

✦ Magical Musings ✦

Laurie Cabot, known as the "official witch of Salem," was born March 6, 1933. This birthdate gives her the life path number 7. Individuals with this life path number are known to travel a spiritual path.

Thus, this potential person who was born on October 12, 1992, would be someone who has an inner spiritual drive and a desire to know the truths of the world. This individual may express this desire through art or other forms of creativity. This person could use photography and writing as a medium to examine the human consciousness or spend free time making wire-wrapped jewelry out of crystals to enhance the spiritual connection.

EXPRESSION NUMBER

Your expression or destiny number is the frequency that explains your desires or goals in life. To find your expression number, you assign a numerological value to each letter in your full birth name.

With your expression number, you will want to find the name that was on your birth certificate, not the nickname that everyone called you or your married name. And make sure to use the full birth name, which includes any middle name that you were given.

Use the following Pythagorean Number Table to find which number is associated with which letter.

1	2	3	4	5	6	7	8	9
A	B	C	D	E	F	G	H	I
J	K	L	M	N	O	P	Q	R
S	T	U	V	W	X	Y	Z	

For example, if your name were Susan Lydia Smith on your birth certificate, you would assign each letter of that name a number as follows:

Susan: S (1) U (3) S (1) A (1) N (5) ... 1 + 3 + 1 + 1 + 5 = 11 (do not reduce further because it's a master number)

Lydia: L (3) Y (7) D (4) I (9) A (1) ... 3 + 7 + 4 + 9 + 1 = 24 ... 2 + 4 = 6

Smith: S (1) M (4) I (9) T (2) H (8) ... 1 + 4 + 9 + 2 + 8 = 24 ... 2 + 4 = 6

Expression number: 11 + 6 + 6 = 23 ... 2 + 3 = 5

This hypothetical Susan Lydia Smith has an expression number of 5. As you'll learn, 5s typically have inner desires and goals to experience all of life itself and feel the freedom of doing just that. She may have a travel blog where she documents all her journeys and adventures, saving each extra dollar for the next plane trip to exotic locales. Susan may be the type of individual who flits from job to job, not staying in one place too long to avoid getting bored.

Soul Urge Number

The soul urge number, sometimes called the heart's desire, tells you what your inner-core self longs for. This number can reveal hidden truths about yourself that not even you were aware of or information about yourself that you had suppressed. The results of this number sometimes do not feel like they match you right away, especially if you are younger, but as you grow and mature, your soul urge number becomes more of who you are as a person.

This number is found by adding only the vowels in your full birth name. The vowels of your birth name, taken together, vibrate at a frequency that reveals your inner self and your core truths, the essential parts of you that you may hide from the world at large.

We will calculate the soul urge number of, again, our hypothetical Susan Lydia Smith, figuring out what she longs for while she bounces from job to job with just her travel blog as her constant companion.

Susan: U (3) A (1) = 3 + 1 = 4
Lydia: Y (7) I (9) A (1) = 7 + 9 + 1 = 17 ... 1 + 7 = 8
Smith: I (9) = 9
Soul urge number: 4 + 8 + 9 = 21 ... 2 + 1 = 3

Susan will have a soul urge number of 3. So, while our hypothetical travel blogger never quite feels settled in one place and enjoys the freedom of moving around, her inner desire is to do something creative. This can be seen reflected in the photos she takes for her blog, which always are shot at unique angles and have great color contrast. She may have even wanted to go to art school after high school, but her parents discouraged her, and instead of pushing for what she really wanted, she got the first job she could find—and we all know by now that the job didn't last more than a couple of months.

PERSONALITY NUMBER

In contrast to your soul urge number, your personality number is found by adding only the consonants of your birth name. The consonants vibrate at a frequency that shows how you express yourself to the world at large. This is the public face you put on when you walk on the street and what people see when they first meet you. Sometimes this number can feel like a surprise if you aren't aware of what aspects of yourself you are portraying. By looking at your personality number, you can find which traits are positive and which natural tendencies you might want to highlight when you are meeting new people or going out on that first date. This way you can make a first impression that is really representative of who you are.

It is back to Susan and her wandering ways. Let's discover what people see when they meet her and how others perceive her.

Susan: S (1) S (1) N (5) = 1 + 1 + 5 = 7

Lydia: L (3) D (4) = 3 + 4 = 7

Smith: S (1) M (4) T (2) H (8) = 1 + 4 + 2 + 8 = 15 ...
    1 + 5 = 6

Personality number: 7 + 7 + 6 = 20 ... 2 + 0 = 2

Susan has a personality number of 2. Now we know why she keeps getting hired even though she hasn't stayed in a job longer than that four-month stint at an accounting firm in Reno. When people meet Susan for the first time, she comes off as trustworthy and honest. People think she is reliable and someone who will stick with the company, no matter what happened in the past. Maybe they look at her travel blog and see all the years of effort and consistency she put in there and think she will give the same to their job. Plus, Susan is just a likeable person, so they should hire her no matter what her resume looks like.

CREATING A NARRATIVE FROM YOUR CORE NUMBERS

Once you have all your core numbers, you can look at them together as a whole and create a narrative or story that explains how each of the numbers is expressing themselves in your life, just like we did for our hypothetical Susan Lydia Smith.

You'll learn more about each number later in this chapter. For now, here's a summary of Susan. With that October birthdate, we can see that she came here to be a spiritual person and to do this through creative means. She likes to move around and enjoys the freedom of life, not liking feeling constricted. Through this freedom she allows herself to open up to the possibilities of the universe and learn new spiritual wisdom and insights.

Susan longs to be creative and show that side of herself, but she isn't focusing on her creative pursuits at the moment, although she might find her way back to them when she is more mature. Instead her main goal in life right now is to find the next paycheck that will fund the next flight to Bali so she can get just the right picture for her blog.

It is easy for Susan to live this lifestyle right now. She knows that, no matter where she ends up, she will find a way to survive financially. She doesn't need much to live off of, and her spiritual philosophy is one of simplicity and moderation. Susan is happy in her life right now—as long as she has her travel blog, anything is possible.

Now create the narrative of your life. Use your core numbers to uncover the secrets of who you are and why you behave the way you do in certain situations. This will help you understand yourself and also your wants and needs. From these numbers you can also discover what partner will fit you best.

Susan would not do well with a long-term partner who has a life path number 6 and prefers to stay at home. Instead, someone with a life path number 3 or 5 would mesh well with her traveling lifestyle. Maybe it would even help Susan to realize that a long-term partner isn't really what works for her desires right now and a couple of one-night stands would be perfect instead.

Tips for Beginners

When figuring out your numbers, it is important to pay attention to the details. This means adding the numbers in a certain order and being mindful of the name you use. Changing the order of addition could give you the wrong number, and you could end up with a personality profile that doesn't match your vibes.

Adding Numbers

When finding your life path number, make sure to add and reduce the day, month, and year separately before adding them together. This will ensure your number is correct. Do not reduce master numbers (11, 22, and 33). When you add the final numbers together, keep reducing until you get either a single pure number or a master number. For example, the following calculations apply to the birthdate June 29, 1984:

June: 6

29: 2 + 9 = 11 (do not reduce further because it's a master number)

1984: 1 + 9 + 8 + 4 = 22 (do not reduce further because it's a master number)

6 + 11 + 22 = 39 ... 3 + 9 = 12 ... 1 + 2 = 3

Special Circumstances with Names

Generally, you will use your birth name in calculating your core numbers; however, this does not mean that the other names you go by don't have any significance. Each name or nickname that you are called adds to the vibratory nature of your energetic field.

It is fun to check what number these names say about you and how people that know you by these different names may view you differently than people who call you by your birth name. This is also a fun exercise to do if you are considering changing your name or perhaps even taking on or hyphenating your partner's name. Does one formation fit better with your personality than the other? Check them out and see what you prefer!

✦ *Magical Musings* ✦ ———

Many witches use magical names when working with spirits and the universe. Before choosing a name, look at the numerology and see if it fits what you want to accomplish. Then figure out if that name will be in harmony with your given name.

Is *Y* a Vowel?

If you have a *y* in your name, you might be wondering if it is considered a consonant or a vowel—should you use it to calculate your personality number or your soul urge number? The answer to this question isn't as simple as you would like. Sometimes *y* is considered a vowel, and sometimes it is considered a consonant.

The rule for how to determine this in numerology is to look at how the *y* sounds. Does it sound heavy and sharp like a consonant? Or, does it sound like it is taking the place of a vowel in the word?

In the example we used earlier, the *y* in *Lydia* is considered a vowel because it sounds just like an *i* and takes the place of an *i* in the name, whereas in the name *Yasmin*, the *y* is considered a consonant.

OTHER MAGICAL APPLICATIONS OF NUMBERS

You do not have to confine numerology to your personal self and profile based on your name and birthdate. Instead, apply it broadly to the world around you or just to your own little corner of the world. The key is to pay attention to numbers wherever they may show up.

HOUSE NUMBERS

Take a look at the address where you live. What does it say about the vibrations of your house or apartment? What about where you work? The places we assign numbers to carry the vibrational frequency of the numbers associated with them.

Adding up the numbers of your address will give you a general feeling for what the energy of the place feels like. If you do not like the frequency that the location is associated with, you can always change it. How can you change your house number without moving, though? Some people simply put an additional number on the inside of their door to shift the numerical vibration of their house.

For example, if your street address is 235, this would reduce to a 1 vibrational frequency. A 1 symbolizes power, but it is also not the best frequency to encourage romantic partnerships. If your address adds up to a 1, you may consider taping the number 1 or 3 on the inside frame of your front door to shift the vibration to a 2 or 4, which will inspire romantic harmony.

If you live in an apartment or condo, consider the different frequencies of both the street address and the apartment number. You can look at these separately and add them together to get a feel for what you are working with. If you live at street address 235, but your apartment number is 1, your place will have a vibrational frequency of both 1 (the apartment number) and 2 (the street address plus the apartment number). This would give the location the qualities of both independence and harmony—a great combination if you want to be the alpha in a relationship.

Life Cycle Numbers

In addition to your core numbers, another number that influences you and the world around you is the year. Every new year, the world at large, as well as you yourself, switch to a new life cycle number. These numbers have a broad effect on the lives that we all need.

To calculate the life cycle year, just add up the numbers in the year. For example, 2018 was an 11 vibrational year, whereas 2023 will be a 7 vibrational year. The whole world will be influenced by this vibration, and you will see shifts that correspond with the numerological energies present.

You, personally, also go through a life cycle year every year. Some numerologists count your new year as starting on January 1, while others count your year as starting on your birthday. Pay attention to your own energy and events of your life to try to determine which way you should calculate your life cycle number.

To find this number for you personally, just add the numbers of your birthdate but switch the current year for your birth year. For example, if you were born December 8, 1990, your life path number would be 3. If the year is 2020, your life cycle year is 6, and if 2021, your life cycle year is 7.

— ✦ *Magical Musings* ✦ —

If you want to create a spell but don't want others to know what it is about, try using a numerological shorthand to identify it. Add up the numerological value of each letter in your desire and create a master number for the spell. You can inscribe this number on a candle or say the spell that number of times to add power.

Your years will cycle through the numbers, sometimes stopping on a master number if you are having a pivotal year, and then cycle back through again. If you look back on the previous years, can you see which years were 9-numbered years, which symbolize endings and completions? How about 1-numbered years, which represent starting new journeys? This is a fun way to look at your life from fresh eyes and see all the cycles you have and will go through.

WHAT EACH NUMBER MEANS

Now that you have calculated your core numbers, it is time to look at what each number represents. Each number has general characteristics that you can interpret and enhance based on the way this number is applied to your personality profile. For example, a 5 as a life path number usually means that you enjoy change and moving around from place to place. If your 5 is found as a soul urge number, you may stay in the same place all your life but dream of exploring the world, and you might like to lose yourself in books describing all the exotic locales that you never end up going to.

Also look if you have a multiple of the same number in your core numbers. This means that the vibration of that specific number has a stronger effect on your personality. For example, if your expression number and personality number are both 1s, you likely desire to be the boss and dominate the world you have made for yourself, and other people will know this about you too. They will see you as someone who is a leader and good at taking control.

It is important to remember when looking at the essence of the numbers to trust your gut and your intuition. Numbers can have different facets, and your inner knowing is what will make it clear how the numbers apply to you or the person you are trying to understand better.

ESSENCE OF 1

The essence of 1 shows through as an individual who has a singular focus on self. They seek to learn and achieve to benefit themselves personally. Although they may seem benevolent at times, any act of giving usually results in some personal reward as well. Achievement, creation, invention, family, and friends are expressions of the 1's ability to achieve and create success. The 1 is loyal, a leader who is fair and given to spurts of amazing generosity. The 1 shows and inspires others by personally demonstrating what he or she is capable of doing as an individual.

── ✦ *Magical Musings* ✦ ──

Witches like to use the phrase "as above, so below" to symbolize how we are all connected in universal oneness. There is one force that runs throughout us and throughout the universe. The acts that we perform on Earth are reflected back to the astral plane, and the motions and occurrences in the astral influence us on in the mortal world. Thus the number 1 is a key theme in witchcraft.

The 1s also tend to be seen as alphas and like to push their way through any situation. This is the number that represents beginnings and new adventures, and sometimes to start something new one must be brave and push in situations where other numbers may hold back. This pioneering and visionary presence is needed to create new ground and new opportunities for the 1, as well as those who come after.

If you have 1 as a core number, see how these qualities of leadership, loyalty, domination, and spunk are expressed. These are the characteristics of someone who can be the head of a *Fortune* 500 company or start a new nonprofit to save the world. As a partner, they will likely take the lead and be loyal to the end.

ESSENCE OF 2

The essence of 2 is filled with the capacity and desire for contact with others. This personality loves individuals, groups, communities, nations, and the world as a whole. The 2 essence is a tireless worker for others who wants to create environments in which people thrive and in which the focus is usually comfort, security, peace, and harmony. The desire to create a better world promotes the ability of the 2 to be diplomatic, empathic, and emotionally sensitive to the unsaid words of others. This in turn creates an astounding ability to welcome in all and then more. "Always room for one more" could be 2's motto.

There is also a natural humility that goes with the 2. This creates a quiet, sometimes obscure, life and an amazing ability to find blessings in the small wonders of life. The only rigidity is in the support of others, which 2 will do with a quiet force few will withstand.

If you have 2 as a core number, see how these qualities of harmony, togetherness, sensitivity, and security are expressed. This is the essence of the nurturing lover as well as the environmentalist who wants to help every sea turtle.

ESSENCE OF 3

The essence of 3 is pure light and fun. The 3 loves to share and inspire joy and happiness. The 3 tends to automatically attract friends and admirers by the droves and draws fun from everyone and everything. Like a happy puppy, the 3 goes through life with ears flapping, tail wagging, and engaging, with a pure joy of being alive.

The 3 essence doesn't recognize tragedy and loss as a reason for depression or self-doubt. It is not really true that the 3 essence is a specialist in escapist behaviors; instead, they see and relate to the silver lining in every situation.

The 3 is also the number of creation and creativity. The 3 tends to express itself as an individual who can manifest new and exciting projects and performances quickly and easily. The essence of 3 is that of taking two separate items and changing them into something new and different. That's why the 3 represents two people coming together and bringing about a child. From two there becomes three. This is the essence of the 3 energy.

—— ✦ *Magical Musings* ✦ ——

The number 3 is an important one for witches. Some witches like to say a spell three times. This is considered to imbue the spell with the energies of the mother, maiden, and crone or the past, present, and future.

If you have 3 as a core number, look how the qualities of joy, happiness, and creativity express themselves in your life. A 3 individual is someone who can find creative solutions to every problem and who finds joy in friendships and relationships.

ESSENCE OF 4

The 4 essence is the pure soul of dependability, structure, loyalty, and trust. In other words, this essence is everything you would associate with a firm, solid expression of the best of values, morals, and traditions. The 4 is a person who is very disciplined—for a cause.

This is a soul essence who upholds the most basic structures or morals of the culture. In the Western world's case, this would be partnership, loyalty, family care, a respectable job, and true patriotism. This soul essence is traditional, not particularly inventive, but very loving. The 4 essence is invested in both needing and giving a consistent and constant support. The 4 essence is inclined to see others' needs before their own and is therefore capable of putting others first when making decisions.

The 4 essence values knowledge and is always learning to avoid a limited point of view and holding on to the past. The 4s tend to understand their likes and dislikes, but they keep this self-knowledge private.

If you have a 4 as a core number, see how the qualities of loyalty, dependability, family, and traditional values express themselves. These are the characteristics of an individual who values family life and will go to a traditional job every day to provide for those that depend on them.

ESSENCE OF 5

The 5 essence is the emotional explorer who is constantly on the move. This essence is restless and freedom-oriented, the "mover and shaker" energy personified. The constant curiosity makes the 5 essence very adaptable to life but not often really changed by it. Something of a free spirit, this essence adds a special liveliness and excitement to any situation it finds itself in.

They are usually ready to move on to the next experience whenever the present one no longer holds their attention or interest. This natural way of expanding means that the 5 essence has an interest in the arts, music, great food, travel, and fine clothes and jewels. To this essence, all these things mean the good life that has been sought, embraced, and fulfilled.

If you have a 5 as a core number, see how the qualities of exploring, adaptability, refinement of taste, and change are expressed in your life. The 5 is usually willing to try any new experience, including under the sheets, and loves surprises that change up mundane life.

ESSENCE OF 6

The 6 essence is the nurturer. They embody a powerful essence of protective friendship, loyal love, a comfy home, and a deep, steady root that gives endless support to others. Deeply connected to the physical and emotional rootedness, the 6 essence carries a deeply comforting, calming, and reassuring quality. They acknowledge that life can be a challenge at times, but through it all, they remain eminently trustable. The 6 essence demonstrates to others how to deal with life's unexpected twists and turns and how to believe in the power of comfort and sustaining love as an ever-present force to balance the impermanence of change.

The 6 essence is inclined to work out of the home, or in a very homey refuge, or in a protecting environment. They may find employment in counseling or in the legal arena, working with laws that protect others. The 6 essence expresses qualities associated with "home" in all aspects of life.

Everyone in 6's life is greeted as a guest or friend and is given stable, loving, parental support. The 6 essence has a great natural compassion and empathy for others and will readily give tremendous love and support to others. That's because deep within, the 6 essence knows he or she is fully protected and secure in the material world.

In relationships, the 6 essence tends to be stable and grounded. They are not likely to cheat and will often stay in a relationship long past its expiration date just because they are comfortable in the partnership.

If you have 6 as a core number, see how the qualities of home life, friendship, steadiness, and support express themselves in your life. These are the characteristics of someone who is calm and nurturing to their friends and who brings a sense of comfort in a world full of chaos.

ESSENCE OF 7

The 7 essence is the most enigmatic, or least knowable, of the numbers. This essence is always alone, preferring to spend time in their inner world, which is usually fairly involved. They often have interests related to science, philosophy, and other pursuits of the intellect. This intellectual relationship is the 7 essence's primary relationship. They often have a difficult time with mundane conversations but will brighten up and speak for hours about theoretical science and philosophical points of view.

Because of their preference for living in their head instead of in the physical world, it may be difficult to really get to know the 7. Speaking about the weather or local politics may cause a 7 to shut down. Instead, finding an interest that is relatable to the 7's highly involved inner world, such as spirituality or theoretical physics, may break the 7 out of their shell and help form a strong and lasting connection.

The 7 essence loves to examine situations and people from every angle. This essence analyzes everything and hates to be drawn into messy human stuff, such as fighting, dirty manual labor, and chaotic environments. Instead, they will hang back from any physical situation and watch it unfold, examining the process and interactions. If asked to help a friend put together a bookshelf, they are more likely to sit back and watch the friend struggle with the process, offering suggestions when they grab the wrong screw instead of wielding the screwdriver themselves.

The 7 essence will automatically be learning how to be alone and, at the same time, fully content and never lonely. As the 7 essence becomes more comfortable with life, much of the fear and longing transforms to courage and the ability to find beauty in the everyday moments of life.

If you have 7 as a core number, see how the qualities of spirituality, mental pursuits, analysis, and aloneness express themselves in your personality. These are the characteristics of the mystic who can spend more time contemplating life's greatest mysteries than remembering that they have a date scheduled in an hour and need to get ready.

— ✦ *Magical Musings* ✦ —

The 7 is a very spiritual number and one that witches focus on in many forms. For example, witches often work on balancing and unblocking their 7 chakras in order to harness more energy and power in their spellwork.

ESSENCE OF 8

The 8 essence can be summed up very simply in these two words: expects success. Imbued with talents for organization and systems of any kind, and further blessed with an affinity for large affairs and events and the personal power to conceive, organize, and direct them, the 8 essence has the love and ability to achieve on a great scale.

The 8 essence will never ask another to work harder, give more, or strive more than 8 essence does. The 8s are tireless workers, direct in their approach and driven by their visions, energized by their imagination and projects, and filled with love when they are creating great things. This essence is a power source of hard work to create good—the party planner who can pull together a gala to support the local children's hospital with just a month's notice.

As life rolls along, the 8 essence will learn tolerance for those who have other, very different qualities, such as the friend whose car is always a mess or the coworker who can't seem to ever find their stapler. They will develop patience with the process, recognizing the goal can only be achieved when the process is well supported.

If you have 8 as a core number, see how the qualities of success, hard work, dedication, and prosperity are expressed in your life. These are the characteristics of the individuals who give their all in every pursuit, from planning the perfect date to making sure their house looks nice.

ESSENCE OF 9

The 9 essence is the expression of universal awareness and universal wisdom. This wisdom can take the form of extraordinary generosity because the 9 essence always feels completely cared for by the universe; because they are well supported, they are capable of supporting others. The 9 essence's great faith in universal abundance enables the 9 to express a very high order of love. This type of love takes the form of sacrifice without martyrdom; sympathy without pity; understanding without arrogance; and service without treating the person served as a needy, lesser being.

The 9 essence longs to have deep personal love, but this essence emanates such an intensely universal, impersonal quality of love that the deep human love is often hard for the 9 essence to really achieve. They have difficulty applying this universal love on an individual level, making it easier for them to love all humanity while finding fault with the partner in front of them. The 9 essence, who is beautiful inside and out and beloved by most, is often moved to share his or her wisdom on social media to connect with the most people, not for his or her ego but to get the wisdom out.

As the 9 essence goes through life, they generally have to be aware of their idealism and how it applies to the world around them. Although doing the "right thing" may seem common knowledge for the 9, others may find this quality difficult to live with and annoying at times. The 9 will easily point out when their friends and partners do not live up to their high standard, such as when a friend walks right past a homeless individual on the sidewalk, not noticing or offering assistance.

If you have 9 as a core number, see how these qualities of universal knowledge, empathy, awareness, and higher love express themselves in your life. These are the characteristics of someone who wants to know everything and will research all possibilities before settling on one choice or one partner in life.

ESSENCE OF 11

The 11 essence embodies a spiritual teacher. In the historical definition of spiritual teacher, the teacher stood on the podium and lectured, encouraged, and enlightened the masses. This is the 11 of yesterday. The 11 essence today still has this love of Source before its love of humanity but tends to express ideals without being accessible as a human being, which can sometimes come off as aloof and distant. But the 11 essence is increasingly evolving in our modern society into a deeply human person who glows with amazing spiritual dimension in the blessed but ordinary muck and mire of human life. They may have a social media account that shows their unique spiritual perspective that can be seen in everyday life, not from a monastery but from the city streets. The 11 essence is a treasure of spiritual teaching and deeply personal human love that ignites the best in all it meets.

As the 11s live their lives, their appreciation for humanity will develop and expand. They will learn to recognize the small miracles of everyday life and the spiritual truths that encompass ordinary tasks. They will be able to apply deep spiritual truths, such as the universal oneness of all, to the world around them and the people they interact with. This is the individual who looks at a bowl of cereal and proceeds to tell you an anecdote for life that changes forever how you view your morning meal.

But the 11 essence is not only about positivity and spiritual truths. There is a backstory here that explains how the 11 is able to have this great wisdom, and it usually involves trials and hardships. The 11s usually go through a crisis or a pivotal act in their lives or relationships that leads them to a higher knowing and understanding of the world around them.

Before going through a trial, the 11 essence will normally express itself in the reduced form of 2. It is when this 2 energy is tested that the 11 of the spiritual teacher emerges and is shaped into the wise essence of this master number.

—— ✦ *Magical Musings* ✦ ——

When you see 11:11 on a clock, this may be a sign that a spirit is trying to contact you. Many witches find that they randomly look at the clock right as these master numbers appear. It may be more than coincidence!

If you have 11 as a core number, see how the qualities of mysticism, spiritual truths, and wisdom express themselves in your life. These are the characteristics of the wise individual who may not tell you all they have had to go through in life, but if you look deep into 11's eyes you will be able to see the old soul that lies beneath the surface.

ESSENCE OF 22

The 22 essence embodies the characteristics of all the other numbers, including the qualities of the 11 essence, combined. As a result, you have someone who understands the laws of the universe and knows that these laws are only useful if they are applied in harmony with nature's laws—a powerful, practical builder of systems and communities. He or she does not build for personal power, ego needs, experimentation, or from personal insecurities. The 22 essence builds to improve existence on the physical level so all else can grow and thrive. This essence is a true believer in the maxim that in order for human growth and potential to ignite, create, and be grand, the practical, physical aspects of life must be in place.

This master number, like 11, usually is preceded by a hardship or crisis that leads to a greater understanding of the world, both spiritually and physically. However, while the 11 takes the knowledge from this difficult time and uses it for deep spiritual growth, the essence of 22 uses the information to create and build a structure that can help others for generations to come. These are individuals who can take a platform and create a thriving community of like-minded individuals who help and inspire each other. These are individuals who could use modern technology to create an app to unite people or form grassroots networks in neighborhoods to help elderly individuals about to lose their homes.

The younger 22 who has not yet been tested expresses itself as a 4. But, as the essence of the number grows and experiences the trials of life, it has the opportunity to learn and evolve.

If you have 22 as a core number, see how the qualities of great wisdom, master building, and universal harmony express themselves in your life. These are the characteristics of the individual who creates a nonprofit that feeds an entire nation or molds a business into a force for good.

ESSENCE OF 33

The essence of 33 expresses itself as a master teacher. Whereas 11 understands the spiritual ways of the universe and 22 builds on these truths, 33 is able to take all the wisdom and spread it to the world. The number 33 is the combination of all the spiritual knowledge of 11 and the understanding of the physical world of 22 expressed in a pure spiritual form. These are individuals who move beyond the local spiritual influence of the 11 and take the platforms and communities created by the 22 to spread information on a global level. At the highest and most evolved levels, the 33 essence expresses itself as gurus who travel around the world spreading messages of peace, harmony, and love.

— ✦ *Magical Musings* ✦ —

The infamous magician Aleister Crowley was born Edward Alexander Crowley. Using his birth name, he has a personality number of 33, that of the master teacher. This fits how society has viewed him perfectly, either for good or bad, because he is known for his work spreading occult knowledge. He was a master teacher who has influenced people and societies around the world even decades after his death.

As with other master numbers, not everyone that has 33 as a core number expresses these qualities. Instead, most express the reduced 6 essence. To fully embody the energy of 33 takes a great deal of spiritual knowledge that most people do not attain in one lifetime.

Individuals who embody the essence of 33 usually go through a hardship or crisis, as with the other master numbers. They are tested or must struggle in some way to enable them to learn the great truths of the universe and become enlightened individuals.

If you have 33 as a core number, see how the qualities of spiritual leadership, altruism, and master teaching express themselves. These are the characteristics of individuals who lead great revolutions, freeing their people from oppression and bringing deep spiritual insights to the world.

POTENTIAL RELATIONSHIPS, BY THE NUMBERS

The first essential step to having a good relationship is to know yourself. Many of us don't slow down and take time to create concrete self-awareness. If you don't know yourself, a truly satisfying relationship with someone else is virtually impossible to create. The insights that numerology offers you will help you build self-awareness.

Once you start to truly understand yourself, you will be able to learn what you really want out of a relationship and what type of person (or people) you are drawn to. Numerology also provides an easy way to peek at the inner longings of your partner to see their essence.

You can compare your numbers with your partner's to see how compatible you are in different areas. This can be done with any of the core numbers, but start with your life path numbers and see how well they work together. If you have a master number as one of your core numbers, use the reduced number to compare your relationship status. For example, if you have 11 as your life path number, look at the relationship for a 2.

+ **1 and 1:** Two 1s together can be explosive at first, so they may have trouble finding a lasting and stable quality. The 1s like to dominate, and individuals in this type of relationship will need to be cognizant of their partner's desire to lead as much as their own. If they find ways to take turns with who makes decisions, this relationship can become a strong and healthy partnership.

+ **1 and 2:** The relationship between a 1 and a 2 can be very successful, since the 1 leads and makes decisions while the 2 balances out and creates harmony in the home. In this partnership, the 1 will want to be mindful of not taking advantage of the 2, and the 2 needs to make sure that his or her preferences are taken into consideration.

+ **1 and 3:** The 1s and 3s make for a fun and dynamic relationship. The spunk and joy of the 3 can be infectious to the 1, and this can make the sometimes serious 1 let down their barriers and have a little fun. In this partnership, each individual should be mindful that too much fun is sometimes a bad thing, and 1 may become tired of the constant excitement. A balance will need to be found between serious work time and fun playtime.

✦ **1 and 4:** A relationship between a 1 and a 4 can be very stable and lead to a long-lasting commitment. Generally, the 1 will take the lead in this type of dynamic and the 4 will provide a stable base for the 1 to come to after a hard day of work. In this partnership, the 4 needs to make sure his or her needs are heard and met; the 4 is not a doormat but rather an individual who has their own desires as well.

✦ **1 and 5:** The 1s and 5s come together in two ways: Either passion sets in or conflict arises. It is "all in" for both numbers, and it's impossible to know what kind of relationship it is going to be until they try it out. A 1 is all about leadership, and a 5 is all about change, so if they are on the same page about what needs to change, things will go smoothly. But, if the 1 is stuck in their ways and not up for different scenery, this relationship may end in a major argument.

✦ **1 and 6:** This relationship will be very harmonious, but, just as between the 1 and the 4, the 1 needs to make sure they are taking into consideration the needs and desires of the 6. The 6 is the ultimate nurturer and also needs to watch out that they do not become codependent and lose their identity to the boldness of the 1.

✦ **1 and 7:** The 1s and 7s have a lot to teach each other, and this relationship can be very rewarding for both parties if they are able to keep an open mind. A 1 can show a 7 how to live successfully in the physical world, while the 7 can show the 1 what the spiritual purpose of living in this world is all about. Close-minded 1s will have a difficult time with the spacey qualities of a 7, but this relationship can work out with patience.

✦ **1 and 8:** The 1 with the 8 is the ultimate power couple. You have the leadership and dominance of 1 energy combined with the prosperity and knowledge of the 8, and you end up with a couple that can be fierce competitors in all aspects of their lives. If you take this pairing to trivia night, they are likely to take it very seriously and may end up winning everything.

✦ **1 and 9:** The 1s and 9s may work well together if their personalities are open to seeing their partner's perspective on each situation, but, if they are stuck in their ways, this pairing will have a hard time taking off. A 1 can learn a lot from the knowledge and experience of a 9, but a 9 also needs to be willing to look at each obstacle from the fresh perspective of the 1.

✦ **2 and 2:** Two 2s in a relationship can be very harmonious and peaceful. This relationship is the type where both keep saying yes and deferring to the other for what they will do. Any major decision that needs to be made may take longer than normal, but, eventually, they will decide where to go for dinner.

✦ **2 and 3:** A 2 with a 3 has the potential to be an exciting relationship. The 3 will bring fun and excitement, while the 2 lends a bit of stability to the process. The 2 in this relationship needs to make sure that their desire for downtime and relaxation is respected by the 3. But a 3 can help the 2 come out of their shell and have new experiences.

✦ **2 and 4:** This relationship can be very harmonious and has the potential to be long-lasting. The 2s and 4s both like stability and consistency. They likely will not have any large fights, but that can mean that passion could also be absent from this relationship. The 2 and 4 may remain in a relationship past its expiration date just because it feels comfortable.

✦ **2 and 5:** The 2s and 5s are at opposite ends of the spectrum. The 2s like stability and harmony, while 5s value change and newness. A relationship between them will be a constant adjustment and struggle but can help widen their perspectives. If both parties are patient and open-minded, it's possible to create a dynamic relationship that enhances the lives of both individuals.

✦ **2 and 6:** Like the 2 with the 4, a relationship between the 2 and the 6 can be very long-lasting and full of a great amount of joy. These two numbers are very comfortable together and can find a nice balance between home life and getting out and experiencing new things. These numbers just need to make sure they are not complacent and that they change up their routine every now and again.

✦ **2 and 7:** A 7 can really open up the world of a 2 in a dynamic way, but the 2 needs to be willing to see life from a new and unique perspective. The 7 may benefit from the stability of the 2 but may also find it conflicting. The surface relationship between the 2 and 7 will be very peaceful and harmonious, but the 2 must remain open-minded for this relationship to last.

✦ **2 and 8:** This relationship has the potential to be great for both parties. The 2 will provide balance and harmony, while the 8 offers growth and opportunities. The 2 will need to make sure to be open to the possibilities that the 8 provides, which may rattle them at first but can eventually lead to a stable footing.

✦ **2 and 9:** The 2 with the 9 is an interesting pairing. The 9 will provide a great deal of wisdom and understanding to the 2, which can help with growth if the 2 is up for a little change. The 9 may appreciate the dependability of the 2 and enjoy the harmony that the relationship can provide.

✦ **3 and 3:** Watch out with two 3s together—this is a recipe for excitement and fun. Two 3s can lead to great dinner parties and exciting date nights. Individuals in this type of relationship just need to watch that they balance out all the fun and excitement and make sure they are not only entertaining each other but are also working to create a lasting relationship.

✦ **3 and 4:** A 3 with a 4 has the potential to be a strong and rewarding pairing. The 3 brings excitement whereas the 4 brings stability. This relationship will have a good mix of excitement and downtime. If both individuals respect the needs of the other, they can endure.

✦ **3 and 5:** This relationship can be very dynamic and exciting. The 3 may be able to hang on for the wild ride of the 5 liking to spice things up with a little change and excitement. There will never be a dull day in the life of this pairing, as both will bring their unique sparks to the relationship. Just watch out for disagreements because they can be just as passionate as both the individuals.

✦ **3 and 6:** The 3s and 6s have the potential to have a stable yet exciting relationship. This is the type of pairing that loves to throw dinner parties in their home, with the 6 being the master of the household and the 3 liking the excitement of friends and parties. If these individuals can find ways to complement each other, this relationship has great possibilities.

✦ **3 and 7:** A 3 with a 7 can lead to a whole new experience for both parties. The 3 may really enjoy the spiritual perspective of the 7 and be willing to travel the universal realms that the 7 lives in. This relationship may not always seem stable, but if the 3 and 7 can find common ground, it can be just as lasting as any even-numbered pairings.

✦ **3 and 8:** This pairing has great possibilities, but only if the 3 is mature and willing to play by the rules of the 8. A mature 8 with an immature 3 will just end in disrespect and a domineering relationship. But, if both parties understand themselves on a deeper level, the joy of the 3 can bring excitement into the life of an 8.

- **3 and 9:** The 3s and 9s in a relationship together can keep each other on their toes. They have the potential to help each other grow and mature, especially if they are young when they first get together. The wisdom of the 9 can grow from the experiences and opportunities that the 3 provides in their daily life.

- **4 and 4:** Two 4s together can be very stable, but the relationship also has the potential to be a bit boring. This couple needs to watch out that they don't get stuck in their routines. One or two date nights of watching movies on the couch is okay, but if that is how every night ends up, this relationship may hit a rut early on.

✦ *Magical Musings* ✦

In witchcraft, the number 4 plays an important role because there are four pillars of witchcraft. Also called the witch's pyramid, these four pillars include to know, to will, to dare, and to keep silent. Although these principles may seem simple at first, they are the backbone behind all witchcraft and guide every witch to do their best.

- **4 and 5:** If a 4 can keep up with the 5, this relationship can be exciting and dynamic. The 4 needs to be open to the idea of new experiences whereas the 5 needs to be okay with several nights at home. This relationship works well if the 4 and 5 each take ownership of their needs and trade off planning activities.

- ✦ **4 and 6:** This relationship has the recipe for a long-term, slow-burn, enduring romance. The 6 will be able to nurture and embrace the sweetness and harmony of the 4. The only pitfall possible in this relationship is if the couple is not able to deal with the changes and chaos that can sometimes pop up. A lost job or a flat tire can put this couple in a tailspin, as both prefer routine and stability.

- ✦ **4 and 7:** A 4 with a 7 will be an interesting pairing. This relationship could be very fruitful for both parties if the 4 is open to the 7's spiritual ways. The 7 doesn't usually mind staying at home, at least with their physical body, because their mind can travel the stars. If the 4 respects the 7's need to explore the mental realms and maybe even partakes in a few meditations every now and then, this can be a great pairing.

- ✦ **4 and 8:** This relationship is a strong pairing. The 8 will shine under the stability of the 4. The 4 needs to make sure that the 8's wishes are respected, but, with the right 8, this relationship will provide the reassurance and guidance that both parties need.

- ✦ **4 and 9:** A 4 with a 9 has the possibility of creating a relationship that is beneficial to both individuals. The 4 can benefit from the knowledge of the 9, and the 9 can gain great clarity from the patience of the 4. The 9 in this relationship needs to make sure they do not dominate the 4 and that the 4 is respected for who they are.

- ✦ **5 and 5:** Put two 5s together and you will never know where they are going to be from one day to the next. This relationship has the potential to be very rewarding if the individuals are mature. Two immature 5s may sell all their belongings and end up penniless in the streets of a foreign country, while two mature 5s may invest their profits from one venture to go start a new adventure overseas.

+ **5 and 6:** The 5s and 6s have the potential to work well together if the 5 can find some grounding in their ways. The 6 can really nurture and help the 5 to grow, but the 6 needs to respect the 5's need for change. If the 6 is up for trying a different restaurant every date night, this relationship can endure for years.

+ **5 and 7:** Put a 5 with a 7 and the possibilities are endless. The 5 will appreciate the different and universal perspective of the 7 and may actually listen while the 7 talks about the existence of aliens and the lost city of Atlantis. This pairing will bring a relationship that may not look "normal" on the surface but will provide interesting adventures and growth for both parties.

+ **5 and 8:** Some tension may exist in the relationship between a 5 and an 8 because the 8 may not appreciate the sometimes quirky nature of the 5. If the 8 can appreciate the dynamic abilities of the 5, this relationship can flourish.

+ **5 and 9:** A 5 with a 9 is a recipe for growth for both parties, but a 9 can get tired of an immature 5 after a few dates. For this relationship to last, both parties need to find a balance between give and take—and this includes in bed.

+ **6 and 6:** Two 6s together create a stable and nurturing relationship. The biggest obstacle in this type of pairing is to make sure each individual is not giving too much to the other.

Watch for indications of a codependent relationship, but otherwise, this combination has the potential for harmony.

✦ **6 and 7:** The combination of the nurturing 6 with the spiritual 7 can lead to a relationship that has the potential for personal growth and new experiences. The 6 will bring some stability and grounding to the 7, while the 7 will help expand the world of the 6 beyond just their home.

✦ **6 and 8:** A 6 can really augment the life of an 8 by nurturing all their hopes and dreams. The 8 will benefit greatly from the 6's influence but should watch out for their own tendencies to spend too much time and attention on their own projects. A mature 8 with a 6 can have a stable and supportive relationship.

✦ **6 and 9:** The 6s and 9s together complement each other nicely. The 6 will help the 9 pursue knowledge, and the 9 will expand the 6's view of the world. This relationship is one that can be healthy for both parties.

✦ **7 and 7:** Put two 7s together and you will have a transcendental experience. A relationship between 7s can be very dynamic and experiential, but both individuals will have trouble staying grounded. Two 7s can turn a typical date into a weekend-long spiritual experience, but both may have trouble getting back to work on Monday.

✦ **7 and 8:** A 7 and an 8 together has the potential to be a rewarding relationship for both parties. An 8 will push a 7 to go further in their pursuits, while a 7 will help the 8 to be open-minded to new—and potentially prosperous—ways of thinking. As long as both parties are open and willing to see the other individual's point of view, this can be a very powerful arrangement.

+ **7 and 9:** The relationship between a 7 and a 9 is somewhat like the two 7s' relationship, but it has the potential for both parties to gain a great deal of wisdom. This couple can also learn more about themselves and the world around them if it lasts.

+ **8 and 8:** Two 8s together can be very hard-core. These individuals tend to focus on their work lives, sometimes at the expense of the rest of their lives. Two 8s together may end up only seeing each other every other week or on a scheduled basis. This relationship may suffer from not being grounded in life outside of work, but if that is what both parties value, this relationship may be ideal.

✦ *Magical Musings* ✦

If you lay the number 8 on its side, it becomes an infinity symbol, or a lemniscate. Lemniscates are common in spellcraft and divination work. Adding the energy of 8 to a spell creates an endless supply of abundance.

+ **8 and 9:** The pairing between an 8 and a 9 can be a wonderful relationship that challenges and expands both parties. The 9 will appreciate the knowledge and gumption of an 8, and the 8 will enjoy the intelligence and sophistication of the 9. This type of combination has the potential to be a power couple in social circles and in business.

✦ **9 and 9:** Two 9s together creates an intellectual experience that others may find annoying and not like to be around. If both 9s are mature this relationship will work out well, but if one or both are immature they may bicker and try to one-up each other, always needing to be right or have the last word.

COMPATIBILITY BETWEEN THE SHEETS

Your core numbers can also tell you about how you and your partner may match up in the bedroom. For this category, look at your and your partner's personality number to see how you express yourself during sex. Also take a look at their soul urge number if you want to know what they are longing for but may not even know it. As with relationships, reduce any master number down to its core number to see how they perform in bed or wherever the mood may strike.

✦ **1:** The 1s are dominant in nature and tend to be bossy in bed. They like to be in control, and they know what they want. A mature 1 may lead their partner into an incredible experience if 1 remembers to share. However, an immature 1 may be selfish and leave their partner unsatisfied. If you are with a 1, make sure you tell them what you want and speak up for yourself. If you are a 1, remember to please your partner first before moving on to your own needs.

✦ **2:** The 2s are all about harmony and peace, and they want that in the bedroom as well. A 2 may have difficulty speaking up for themselves and really telling their partner what they are looking for. The 2s may suffer through years of boring or awkward sex just because they don't want to cause disharmony by telling their partner what they really need. If you are a 2, make sure to speak up and let your partner know what you want. If you are with a 2, encourage them to be open and honest.

✦ **3:** The 3s are fun to be around, and that includes under the sheets. A 3 can be playful and will want to have fun while having sex. A mature 3 who knows what they want will not be boring and may lead you into adventurous situations that you never thought would interest you. If you are a 3, be yourself and enjoy sex. If you are with a 3, try to be open and honest with them. If you aren't willing to try the new sex toy your 3 brought home, say something—otherwise, just go for it and enjoy the ride.

✦ **4:** The 4s can be a bit boring and predictable in the bedroom. Once they know what they want, they will perform the same act each and every time. A 4 would do well to let loose a little and let their partner lead them in new and different directions. If you are a 4, see if you can be open and try something new every now and then. If you are with a 4, don't pressure them to go beyond their limits, but see if they would be willing to change things up, at least on occasion.

✦ **5:** You never know what to expect when you come across a 5 in the bedroom. They can be wild and like to change things up, sometimes in the middle of the act. If you are a free-flowing type of person, this may the perfect partner. They will provide a challenge to anyone who is more traditional and just prefers the missionary position. If you are a 5, go have some fun, but make sure your partner is up for that change of pace before introducing a new obstacle, or person, in the bedroom. If you are with a 5, speak up if you are uncomfortable—otherwise, have fun!

✦ **6:** If you want to be loved and nurtured in the bedroom, look for a 6. These individuals put the love in lovemaking. They can be very gentle and kind, making sure their partner is feeling safe and secure before jumping into the act. If you are a 6, make sure you get taken care of as well. It is good to give, but don't forget to receive. If you are with a 6, enjoy yourself, but make sure they get the love they need reciprocated.

✦ **7:** The act of sex with a 7 has the potential to be a transcendental experience. These individuals will benefit from the *Kama Sutra* and any text that relates sex to a spiritual endeavor. Before getting between the sheets with a 7, know that this is not just a physical act for the individual but something that is deeper and more personal. If you are a 7, let yourself enjoy the act of sex and don't take it too seriously.

The pressure to make everything into a spiritual experience may be too much for some partners to handle.

✦ **8:** The 8s tend to go with the flow in the bedroom and are willing to both try something new or stay with the same old positions. An 8 will be reassuring if you need that but will also tell you what they need if you are being too gentle. If you are with an 8, be open to their honesty and trust that they are telling you the truth. If you are an 8, keep an open mind and let your partner take charge sometimes.

✦ **9:** If you find yourself between the sheets with a 9, especially a mature 9, expect to learn something new. If they want to be an expert in sex, they will learn everything possible and then proceed to teach you in a pleasurably excoriating way. If you are a 9, go ahead and learn all you can about sex. Your partner will appreciate it. If you are with a 9, let them show you something new.

Using Numerology for Love

As you've learned, numbers and their vibrations influence every aspect of your life. Take the power and knowledge of numerology and use it to learn about who you are and what you want for yourself. Are you comfortable with stability and don't want anything new or exciting popping up in your life? If so, you may want to stay away from a 5. However, if you live for adventure and excitement, a 5 may be just the right number for you.

Information is power, and once you know how to use numbers to reveal fascinating information, the world is your aphrodisiac oyster. Know what you want and then go out and get it!

— ✦ *Magical Musings* ✦ —

Witches wanting to master the Tarot de Marseille deck should work on learning their numerology. Unlike the Rider Waite deck, this type does not contain any detailed pictures on the "pip," or numbered, cards. Knowing what numbers mean is a quick way to interpret the cards.

— *Chapter 2* —

PALMISTRY:

THE MYSTICAL POWER OF HANDS

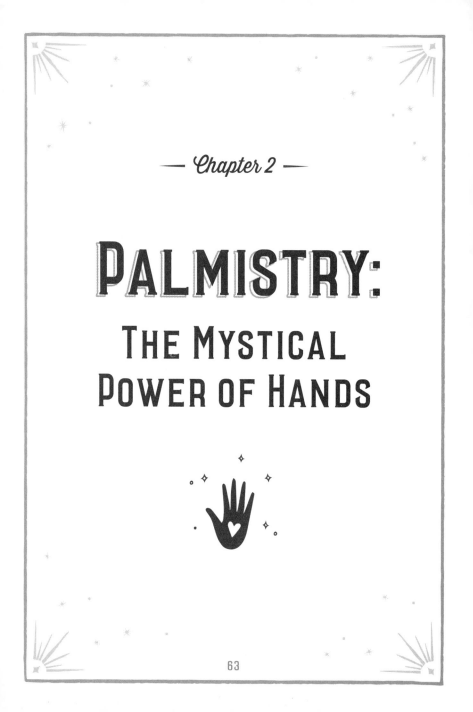

It's often said that the eyes are the windows to the soul, but in many ways, it's the hands that offer the greatest insights into who you are and what you can become. As distinctive as the genetic code that sets you apart from every other individual on the planet, your hands contain unique lines that tell a personal story. No two individuals are the same when it comes to palms and fingerprints, not even identical twins.

By following the lines of your hands and decoding the messages written on your palms, you can gain a better understanding of who you are at your core and what you really want out of life and relationships. You can use this knowledge to make decisions about yourself and your relationships. Check out a potential partner's palms and ask yourself if your heart lines indicate a good match. Are your hand sizes compatible? Do you need a partner who is methodical and takes their time with decisions? If so, someone with smaller hands may be a challenge for you. Do you have similar Venus mounts, showing the potential for passion in the bedroom? Your future is truly in your hands.

Introduction: What Is Palmistry?

Prized as a sacred art in ancient Egypt, India, Italy, and Greece, palmistry has evolved into a powerful intuitive practice that focuses on reading and extracting meaning from the lines, textures, shapes, and idiosyncrasies of your hands—not the palm alone but also the fingers, knuckles, wrists, mounts (fleshy areas), joints, and overall hand shape. Palmistry can reveal the past, but as one of the oldest forms of divination (predicting the future), it also reveals possibilities that lie ahead. Through palmistry, you can discover the blueprint for your life and gain insight into the lives of others around you. The paths on your hands could correlate to paths you've already chosen and indicate others that you might choose to take. In the palm creases and other markings, you will discern a vast world of spiritual—and romantic—possibilities.

✦ *Magical Musings* ✦

The famed *Malleus Maleficarum*, or the witch hunter's book, describes checking for markings on the body that were thought to denote a person as a witch. Individuals during the famed witch hunts were sometimes shaved to look for these indications, which were thought to be charms sewn under the skin.

As it is practiced today, palmistry offers a complete personality profile, including major life choices, challenges, and opportunities. Through connecting with the hands of another individual, you can get a sense of what they may be like as a partner or a lover. Just the gentle physical touch of palmistry—the instant connection generated—can offer an insight into whether there will be a spark between you and your potential partner. What better way to see if someone may be a match than to ask if you can read their palms? Use your intuition to see if there is any spark when you touch their hand and trace their lines!

The Basics of Palmistry

Each person's palms have six major lines, although these lines vary tremendously in their shape, texture, and length. These are the heart line, head line, life line, health (Mercury) line, creativity (Apollo) line, and fate (Saturn) line.

Heart, Head, and Life Lines

+ **The heart line** can tell you about emotional life, including passions, insecurities, and fears. It also indicates potential for love or marriage and is sometimes incorrectly referred to as the marriage line. (Since it encompasses more than just marriage, it is traditionally called the heart line.)

+ **The head line** can provide you with a clearer picture of mental abilities, career or business acumen, and potential for success.

- **The life line** is more than just an indicator of how long a person will live. This line also speaks to personal longevity, stamina, and vitality.

Mercury, Apollo, and Saturn Lines

- **The Mercury line** carries information about health (especially of the central nervous system, which is the messenger system in the body). This line may also show a spirit of adventure and levels of curiosity.

- **The Apollo line** demonstrates potential for successful development of special talents, creativity, and life energies.

- **The Saturn line** is the fate line. It can tell what fate has in store and whether a person is willing or able to accept the responsibilities that will come with whatever fate deals to a person in life.

Special Markings Beyond the Lines

Besides the lines on your hand, there are other special markings that carry meaning in palmistry. Each marking has a potential interpretation that relates to a challenge or obstacle you may face.

One such marking is called a cross or tassel. After a palm reader examines the depth of your lines, they will move on to evaluate their unique characteristics. For instance, your life line could have several crosses around it; this could definitely point to some major life obstacles you've had (or will have) to overcome.

Time is then determined in specific increments along each line, and these markings (documented on palmistry charts) are general indicators of when events did or could happen. It's not an exact science, of course; palmistry thinks of your opportunities in life coming in increments or units of time rather than on specific dates. It's not realistic to expect a reading that says you will find the perfect mate on a Thursday in January, ten years from now. Palmistry can tell you during which period of your life you have the greatest chance to find lasting love and happiness, though.

A Two-Handed Proposition

A palm reader will also consider the overall size, shape, and texture of the hands. For instance, long, thin hands generally indicate that a person is creative and intuitive, while shorter, stubbier hands typically connote a hardworking or athletic type of person.

—— ✦ *Magical Musings* ✦ ——

Many palmists agree that the lines on your palms change as you go through life even though your fingerprints do not change. For that reason, you might choose to read and record the changes in your palms over a long period of time as you age, achieve personal and career goals, and evolve spiritually. Jot notes in your grimoire or personal journal to track these changes.

Both hands must be read to achieve the fullest picture of where you've been and where you're going in life. Your primary, or dominant, hand (usually the one you write with) is often the first to be read. This hand will reveal how well you've been able to meet the challenges or opportunities presented in your minor hand. You'll notice lots of similarity between the hands, with slight to moderate variables on the lines.

Your right brain, which recognizes patterns and understands the relationships between objects or ideas (lateral thinking), controls your left hand. Your left brain, the part involved with reason, logic, and language (linear thinking), controls your right hand. Some palmists associate the left hand/right brain with the feminine and receptive aspects of your personality, while your right hand/left brain reflects the masculine and extroverted aspects.

How to Find a Good Reader

If you want a personal and insightful palm reading, find a professional palmist—someone who is passionate about the work and who truly knows what he or she is doing. There are three types of palm readers: the expert, the novice, and the charlatan. While you may decide to visit the expert or the novice, you clearly want to stay away from the charlatan.

The Expert

An expert palm reader likely will have conducted thousands of readings, possibly for many years—perhaps even for celebrities, high-profile clients, or even law enforcement. While these readers can be quite accurate, they can also be very expensive—with some charging $700 or more for a single session. Choose an expert only if you can afford it and are looking for a high-quality reading.

THE MAGICAL NOVICE

The novice reader likely will be fairly new to the art of palm reading. Although his or her service can be priced more appropriately, such a reader may lack the skill necessary for an in-depth, intuitive, and interpretive reading. Still, novices can provide accurate readings of your life overview and potential. Novices typically charge anywhere from $15 to $70 for a reading that lasts between fifteen and thirty minutes. More often than not, these readers can be found at local psychic fairs and online.

✦ Magical Musings ✦

For your next coven meeting or even a get-together with friends, why not hire a palm reader to come and tell you what your lines reveal? Getting your palm read is a great way to learn the process and more about yourself.

THE CHARLATAN

Sadly, there are charlatans everywhere who are more skilled at pretending to read palms than actually reading them. They know enough to skim the surface of the topic and offer a few meaningful details, but their intent and focus is to constantly request "donations" for candles, additional prayers, and the like.

Initially, this type of reader might charge a small amount to start the reading and then hike the cost by telling you that you have an "evil eye" or some kind of curse on you. To remove it, they offer a veritable laundry list of other psychic services they want you to purchase—naturally, there's a fee for each.

Another hallmark of charlatans is that they typically read only one hand and only the three major lines (heart, head, and life), as opposed to a legitimate reader who will examine all your lines to give you a comprehensive look at your life, accomplishments, and potential.

The Benefits of Learning to Read Palms Yourself

You can also learn to read your own palms or others' palms. Just like in any other arcane art or discipline, regular practice gives you greater understanding and helps you gain proficiency. You don't have to be a psychic to become a palmist—all you need is a receptive mind and the willingness to be honest with yourself and others. Don't fear acknowledging what you see. If it's challenging, explore that challenge. Remember that the future is all about potential and choice.

Since you know yourself best, you might recognize challenges and discover solutions faster on your own palm than someone else could. Many people consider their romantic relationships private, and reading your own palm allows you to keep what you learn to yourself.

Reading Others' Palms Can Lead to Greater Connection

Reading the palms of friends, family members, and even potential love interests can greatly improve your connection to those people. For example, you might modify the way you communicate with a person based on what you see in their palms and discover about their personality. A quick glance at your potential partner's hands may reveal that their palms are long while their fingers are short, indicating fire-shaped hands. With this information, you may be better off suggesting a date night at an amusement park full of adventure and excitement instead of a quiet dinner at a romantic restaurant.

—✦ *Magical Musings* ✦—

If you have developed your third eye, or clairvoyant sight, you may start seeing auras when looking at palms during palm readings. Oftentimes you can see a slight energy around the hand, especially if it is against a white or black cloth.

How to Read Palms

Before you pick up the hand of the stranger sitting next to you and start peering down at their palm, it would be wise to ask permission. Some people are not comfortable with divination and may feel uncomfortable if you start telling them all the secrets that they like to keep hidden. And, many people fear that when you start reading their palms, you will tell them that they are about to die or inherit some devastating disease. Put the individual you are about to read for at ease and let them know that your palm reading is just showing general characteristics and cannot pinpoint exact information, just tendencies. If they give you permission, you're free to move ahead.

To start a palm reading, it is easiest to begin with an overall assessment of one entire hand, including size, color, thickness, texture, and movement. Take your time so you don't miss anything that might have relevance to your reading. This is also your opportunity to really feel the hand of the individual, see if you are drawn to them and if there is any chemistry forming between you. Here are specific things to start looking for when examining the overall structure of the hand:

+ **Size.** In general, people with small hands tend to act quickly and perhaps impulsively; those with *very* small hands are generally free, independent-minded thinkers. Those with larger hands tend to be more methodical and thoughtful about their big decisions in life. People with average hands are easygoing; they react according to each situation and its own unique circumstances and are not as predictable.

- **Color or consistency.** Color represents life or vitality. If the palms are pale—white, gray, or even bluish—it definitely indicates health challenges (most likely circulatory in nature). Red hands mean quick to anger; yellow, jaundiced hands mean a pessimistic outlook; and pink hands mean a well-balanced and healthy outlook.

- **Thickness.** Tilt the hand sideways and look at its width. Is it thin or thick? Thick hands belong to easygoing, noncompetitive people; thin hands belong to goal-oriented, driven, or ambitious people who are on a specific mission in life.

- **Texture.** Fine, soft skin indicates refined tastes and usually belongs to the culturally or artistically inclined. Firm skin shows a healthy blend of physical and intellectual pursuits. Coarse, rough, or scaly skin indicates a more adventuresome, outdoorsy type for whom gloves (and personal well-being) are an afterthought.

- **Movement.** How does the hand move? Does it seem flexible? If it is, the person is also likely to be flexible in his or her thinking and general demeanor. A general rule of palmistry is that the stiffer the hand, the stiffer the demeanor. Have you ever noticed a person with hands so stiff they almost seem mechanical? People with hands this stiff typically have difficulty expressing themselves and may keep their emotions private, not willing to share their deepest thoughts or cry during that emotional scene in your favorite movie.

- **Hair.** A lot of hair on the back of a man's hand reveals an individual who is confident and may have alpha tendencies, whereas male hands that are soft and hairless frequently belong to a man who is more introverted and private. Women with hair on the backs of their hands tend to be highly assertive. Women with hairless hands often seem calmer.

✦ **Pinkie.** Look at the fourth finger (the pinkie, or little finger) as it relates to the hand. Is it farther apart than the other fingers? Usually, a little finger that points outward and is spaced significantly apart from the third finger means that the person has a quick temper and is not to be reckoned with when upset. If the index finger seems to be spaced farther apart from the other fingers on the hand, the person has strong leadership potential and can be a trendsetter.

Make a note about each of the characteristics you've observed. As you get deeper into the lines, ridges, and mounts of the hand, you'll want to look back at your initial assessment to see if you can make any further connections or conclusions.

Check Out Hand Shape

The general shape of the hand tells a palm reader a lot about general character. The easiest way to get a quick read on someone is to look at the shape that his or her hands form and to correlate that shape with a personality type. In palmistry, there are four basic shapes and one hybrid, or mixed, shape.

✦ *Magical Musings* ✦

Witches recognize the elements in every aspect of their work, and that includes hand shapes. Each type of hand represents one of four elements that the ancients believed composed all matter of our world: Conical hands are said to be air hands; pointed hands are water hands; spatulate hands are fire hands; and square hands are earth hands.

The Conical | AIR HAND

Conical hands seem round, with square palms and long fingers that have a lanky, sometimes bony, appearance. A person with this hand shape has a deep appreciation for the arts. If the hands feature lots of curved lines, the person is an artist. Quiet, sensitive, and imaginative, the person seeks solace through music, art, literature, and love. The conical hand is called the air hand, since this element most closely captures the free spirit of individualism associated with this hand shape. The person with this hand type enjoys having many friends but will be quite selective when seeking a partner. Also, the person likely sticks to the moral high ground.

The Pointed | WATER HAND

The pointed, or water, hand has a narrow palm with long, delicate, and tapered fingers. These fingers characterize water hands and are memorable if you think of them pointing to spiritual truths. This is why the pointed hand is often referred to as the psychic hand— and the vast majority of those who have pointed hands possess psychic or intuitive ability. If the hands are pointed but the person feels a lack of psychic ability, perhaps the person has psychic powers not yet tapped into. Intuition and creative energy are probably waiting for the person to learn more about them so their benefits can be enjoyed.

People with this type of hand typically have tremendous compassion or empathy for others, as well as deep sensitivity and intensity. A person with water hands is highly romantic, responsive to aesthetics, fond of gifts, attracted to sensuality, and bored by routine.

The Spatulate | FIRE HAND

If a hand has a long palm but short fingers, it is called the spatulate, or fire, hand. This hand shape indicates that a person is action-oriented and loves unusual adventures; it's not unlike this person to pack bags and head to India for a spell at an ashram and the next week wander around the market towns of Italy's hill country. This person likes variety and excitement in all areas of life, including the bedroom.

An explorer of people, places, and ideas, this person is daring, energetic, and fearless, often challenging the ideas or positions of others who aren't as open-minded. This person's energy is boundless and tends to leave others breathless, unable to catch up. Spatulate hands are called fire hands since that element most closely captures the personality traits of vitality and dynamism.

The Square | EARTH HAND

An earth hand appears to form a perfect square—a square palm with short fingers. If the hand is square and smooth, the person is easygoing, has a practical nature, and possesses a realistic outlook on life. The person is rooted in the routines of daily life. Friendly and outgoing, the person has a tendency to evaluate every situation as black or white, with little left to interpretation. Still, because the person is so sensible and levelheaded, family and friends regularly seek their help to mediate or settle volatile situations. These people excel in tackling large and difficult projects so are most often drawn to careers that require hard work and persistence.

Because these people are practical and down-to-earth, they are said to have earth hands. The well-padded earth hand also symbolizes a warm, passionate, energetic nature—someone who enjoys the earthly pleasures of food, drink, and passionate indulgences. A thin, square hand, though still an earth hand, suggests less passion and lower libido, while a hard hand often belongs to those who are less flexible and demand more of others.

The Mixed Hand

Although it's quite a rarity, every once in a while you'll see a hand that has elements of two or more of the four shapes and types. Palmists call these hands mixed. For an accurate reading of a mixed hand, you'll need to look for the dominant feature of the hand.

For instance, if you see that the palm itself is basically square but the fingers are long, it could mean that the person seems, by outward appearance, to be dreamy and intuitive but that inwardly they are actually strong, practical, and even minded. If all seems balanced in the hand, your mixed-hand person is completely versatile and has a steady, go-with-the-flow kind of attitude. Both temperaments have their positive and negative sides, but there is much to learn from the mixed-hand, balanced individual.

Major Lines of the Hand

The six major lines—the life, head, heart, health, creativity, and fate lines—are formed even before you are born, and they change throughout your life in response to stress and illness and according to your actions, which in turn create life changes.

Life Line

The life line, located close to the head line, makes a loop around the thumb. It speaks to a person's longevity, stamina, and vitality. A curvy line indicates a lot of energy, whereas a long, deep line suggests a healthy, long life imbued with energy. Or, if there are two or more life lines, the person is surrounded by positive energy and abundant vitality.

Because it lies so near to the mount of Venus, the life line can provide many hints about a person's love life. The life line represents health, so a strong one shows that a person has much passion to give, while a weak one points to a limitation in the amount of energy that a person has to give to physicality.

LIFE-LINE INDICATORS FOR LOVE

If a life line makes a wide sweep across the palm, leaving room for a large mount of Venus, the person has a great deal of love to give and energy to put to use in the sexual arena. The person is likely extroverted and outwardly directed. On the other hand, a life line close to the thumb constricts the mount of Venus and shows a lower sex drive.

Head Line

The head line, located between the first finger and thumb, crosses the midpalm horizontally. The head line can provide you with a clearer picture of the mental abilities, career or business acumen, and potential for success. A straight line indicates deep, clear thinking, while a sloping curved line suggests high creativity.

HEAD-LINE INDICATORS FOR ROMANCE

The head line will also give you clues about romantic relationships. First, compare the head and heart lines. If the head line is heavier than the heart line, the person will look for a partner who can be a good companion and who gives mental stimulation. The person will think before acting on sexual feelings. If the heart line is heavier than the head line, it is just the opposite. The person will be ruled more by feelings and need for passion.

If the head line is straight across the palm, the person is practical and realistic about love and has a less romantic view of things. There is a tendency to be more traditional about social standards. If the head line drops downward to the mount of Luna, the person is more romantic about love, and the bigger the dip downward, the more imagination and illusion play a role in the person's hopes and dreams.

Heart Line

The heart line is located on the little-finger side of the hand where it crosses the palm on its way toward the first finger. The heart line reveals aspects of emotional life, such as insecurities, fears, and passions. It also indicates potential for love or marriage and is sometimes incorrectly referred to as the marriage line. A feathered heart line can suggest a fickle, flirtatious individual. A heart line that originates under the middle finger indicates a tendency to be materialistic and selfish in the affairs of the heart.

The heart line is a good place to start when looking at a person's palm to see what the relationships will be like. This line describes both feelings and passion, and it shows how well a person manages to bond emotionally with others. If the heart line is long, deep, and without blemishes, the person is a devoted friend, secure in relationships, and has an affectionate and loyal nature.

HEART-LINE INDICATORS FOR LOVE

Here are the features that you should look for when reading the heart line for love potential:

+ **Chains and islands:** Feelings are changeable and short-lived. The person wants intimacy but fears commitment so sometimes wavers and is insecure. Other people may see this person as cold and unapproachable.

+ **Shape of the line:** If there is a straight heart line, the person is very cool and rational and has a strong mental image of what he or she wants and is willing to wait for it. Generally, this is the type of person who makes decisions based on what makes sense. If there is a curved heart line, the person is more emotional, moved by thoughts and desires, and willing to move more physically and aggressively toward goals.

+ **Space between head and heart lines:** If the space is wide, the person is tolerant and willing to live and let live. If the space is narrow, the person is secretive and ill at ease in many social situations because it is hard to express feelings.

Also check where the heart line ends. If it tapers off under Saturn (the middle finger), the person is a very physical person, one who is controlled by the rationality of Saturn rather than by sheer romance. If the heart line ends under Jupiter (the first finger, next to the thumb), the person's love life will have a strong component of an idealized view of a partner (or the love affair may be with all of humanity). The person is loyal, but this may veer over into possessiveness.

If the heart line ends between Jupiter and Saturn, the person can balance the forces of head and heart. The person is warm and loving but also can be logical and practical about a partner.

Saturn, or Fate, Line

The Saturn line stretches through the center of the palm to the base of the middle finger (the Saturn mount). The mythical god Saturn ruled duty, work, and security, so it makes sense that the Saturn line (also called the line of destiny) reveals the role of career and responsibility in the person's life. It shows the direction of life and indicates ability to exert control over it and ambition to achieve goals. The fate line also gives insight into how others view the person.

Additionally, the fate line shows relationships that affect the person's life. Relationships are seen in the lines of influence that rise up from the mount of Luna to meet the fate line, and they can be marriages, important friendships, and business partnerships. (Lines of influence are any lines that run parallel to or across major lines.)

The line of destiny mirrors the effort the person puts into creating an ideal life. It gives information about the person's career, ambition, material well-being, personal success, and fulfillment of goals. The line of destiny is the central element of the hand, supplying stability to the other lines because it connects the intuitive and practical zones of the palm. It shows how one acts, uses one's abilities, controls one's environment, and deals with influences.

Other Lines

The palm reveals information about a person in other lines (and in patterns) as well. The Mercury line, for example, runs from the thumb side of the midpalm across to the little finger. It discloses information about health (and especially the central nervous system, which is the messenger system in the body). This line may also show a spirit of adventure and a healthy curiosity. The Apollo line runs up from the midpalm to the ring finger and demonstrates potential for successful development of special talents, creativity, and life energies.

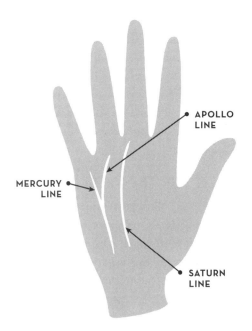

APOLLO LINE

MERCURY LINE

SATURN LINE

EXAMINE KNUCKLES AND ANGLES

Make a fist and closely examine the ridges of your knuckles where they form peaks. A full "mountain range" with peaks and valleys shows a person who has good health, is adventuresome, and fights for his or her beliefs. If your knuckles are smooth and even, you are intuitive, impulsive, and dreamy. If they are knotty and rough looking or heavily ridged, you are extremely decisive and not easily swayed by hard-luck stories. Tiny bumps on the knuckles connote a shy, introverted personality.

INSPECT QUALITIES OF THE PALM LINES

After you examine the general shape of the hand, look at the palm and study the main lines. Lines basically come in four different varieties: deep, clear, faint, or broken. While not completely conclusive until the rest of the palm reading has been completed, the qualities of the palm lines can tell you a lot about the basis or foundation of the person's life. Here are some examples:

+ **Deep lines** indicate a person who is full of life and who is certain or direct about their needs and desires. These people have absolutely no difficulty in attaining their goals in life—and they don't let anyone or anything get in the way!

+ **Clear, easy-to-read lines** that are plain to see but not exceptionally deep typically belong to peace-loving, even-tempered people. These individuals are often the peacemakers in their families, and others look to them for fair and objective insights.

+ **Faint lines** appear in individuals who frequently have lots of nagging health problems, some of which can be caused by years of worry or indecision. Often timid and reserved, these people would rather have others lead them in particular situations; they hate having to take action, especially for their own well-being—they prefer others take care of them.

+ **Broken lines** indicate abrupt or traumatic changes in life. A broken line coming off the life line can mean a major shift in lifestyle or personal well-being. A broken line off the heart line may mean a dramatic change in relationship status, such as divorce or separation.

+ **Long lines** on the palm mean that the person has well-developed interests and pursues them with a passion, while short lines generally mean that the person has many different interests and can be intensely involved with each one—until the next opportunity presents itself.

+ **Horizontal lines** on the palm generally mean conflict or separation.

- ✦ **Vertical lines** point to a tendency toward people pleasing.

- ✦ **Double lines** mean that the person has spiritual guidance in the form of an ancestral spirit, spirit guide, or angel—and this guidance pertains to the area of life that the double lines are closest to (either heart, head, or life line).

— ✦ *Magical Musings* ✦ —

If you spot the secret cross—also known as the mystic cross—on a palm, it is a sure sign that you are in the presence of a natural-born witch. This cross or *x*-shape is located between the head and the heart lines. It does not touch the fate line, but instead is located under the mount of Apollo.

Observe Other Palm Markings and Patterns

In addition to major lines, the palm contains lots of smaller lines and other markings. There may be tiny crisscrossed lines, loops, and other lovely little patterns. No matter how incidental these shapes and patterns may seem, the hands have carried these markings since about the third month of fetal development inside the mother's womb.

Notice the Ridges

First, take a look at the overall texture of the palm in order to get a suitable starting point for reading the ridges and patterns contained in the palm. If the ridges in the palm are smooth and soft to the touch, the person likely has refined tastes and is the quiet and sensitive type. If the ridges are wider and deeper, creating a rougher texture, the person is athletic, action-oriented, and has a positive, outgoing attitude.

While it's possible for hands to have no visible patterns, most hands have at least one type of pattern, and a high percentage of hands have several.

Look for Shapes in the Patterns

Now that you have a good sense of the feel and texture of the palm, take a deeper look at the skin patterns on it. Do they form any particular shapes?

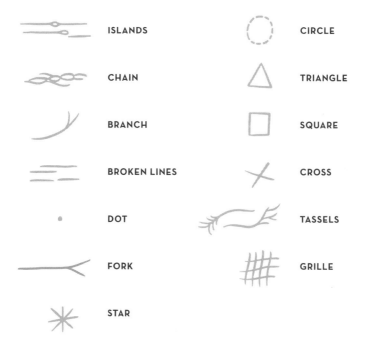

ISLANDS	CIRCLE
CHAIN	TRIANGLE
BRANCH	SQUARE
BROKEN LINES	CROSS
DOT	TASSELS
FORK	GRILLE
STAR	

There are thirteen basic markings that can appear on the palm of the hand, and each has a special meaning:

1. **Chains:** Someone who is bound by worry.

2. **Islands:** Loss through difficulty or challenge.

3. **Dots:** Indication of a surprise or a shocking event.

4. **Branches:** Rising branches are a sign of good fortune; branches falling toward the wrist are a sign of potential failure.

5. **Broken lines:** A shift or change in life, or an inability to see things through.

6. **Forks:** Choices pertaining to whichever major line it is closest to (heart, head, life, health, creativity, and fate).

7. **Circles:** Usually predict great fame and fortune; however, you will rarely encounter them.

8. **Triangles:** Portend great psychic or spiritual abilities.

9. **Squares:** Ability to teach, motivate, or inspire others.

10. **Crosses:** Obstacles or blockages on the way; burdens that may hold a person back from achieving dreams.

11. **Tassels:** Represent scattered energies, weariness, or unmanifested ideas.

12. **Grilles:** Look like hash marks, both vertical and horizontal; represent lots of starting and stopping with respect to life's endeavors.

13. **Stars:** The most auspicious markings on the palm; people with stars usually achieve tremendous fame—or lasting notoriety.

Take Note of Loops

Loops, a type of palm markings, are typically found on the webbing between fingers and on finger mounts (the puffy underside of the knuckles of the hand). Loops of vocation or career, found between the ring and the middle finger, show how dedicated a person is to career. If the loops are large and open, the person is probably open to others' input. If small and refined, the person is likely an entrepreneurial spirit who prefers solitary work.

Loops of bravery or courage are found just above the joint area of the thumb, near the thumb webbing. If the person has one of these, they are fearless in life's pursuits.

Loops of humor or good cheer occur between the index and middle finger and point to a healthy sense of humor that draws others, while a loop on the Luna mount (the outside part of the palm between the pinkie and the wrist) shows a marked ability to communicate with animals and nature.

Find Shapes Predicting Creativity

If the hand has several skin ridge patterns that seem to flow into each other to form a triangular shape, that shape is a focal point for creative energy. If the person has a triradius marking on the index finger mount, it typically means that the person focuses creative energy on leadership; if it occurs near the third finger mount, the person is much more intellectual.

Whorls (unusual circular skin patterns) indicate future greatness in creative endeavors. If the person writes, creates art, or performs for audiences, search for the unique markings that signal intense artistic talent, for example a whorl of music (typically found on the Venus mount, which is the padded section near the thumb) or a whorl of Luna (found on the Luna mount).

Check Out the Percussion Area

Turn the hand sideways and examine the outer lateral edge (the area between the wrist and the pinkie). This area is known as the percussion, and it is wide enough to span three major mounts of the hand.

When the percussion is tapered, it sticks out just below the little finger and then tapers off until it reaches the wrist. If the percussion area is tapered as just described, the person possesses an overly active mind. Relaxing and going with the flow might be difficult. If the hand features a curved percussion, the person has lots of creative ability, although they might choose to use it in practical professions such as engineering. Straight percussions are rare and connote someone who doesn't waste time on artistic pursuits.

— ✦ *Magical Musings* ✦ —

When learning to move and feel energy, oftentimes a witch will work with their hand chakras. Chakras are centers in the body where energy tends to pool and collect. Most people are aware of the seven main chakras, but there are actually numerous chakras located throughout the body and around the aura of every individual. The hand chakras are easy to learn to activate and work with. Start by rubbing your hands together quickly and then pull them apart. This will open your hand chakras and allow you to sense energy using your palms. Once your hand chakras are open, try moving them over different objects and pay attention to the sensations you feel.

LOOK AT THE MOUNTS OF THE PALM

The palm contains nine mounts (the fleshy raised areas on the palm), such as the mount of Luna and the mount of Venus. Palm mounts reveal personal characteristics, natural abilities, and traits. If you are interested in where dominant energies are directed, look for the largest raised area on the palm.

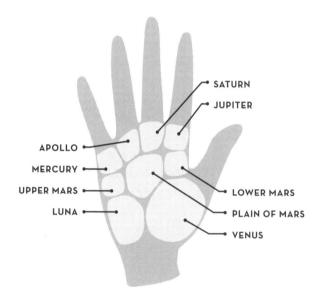

Mount of Venus

The mount of Venus, located at the base of the thumb, indicates how deeply or passionately a person loves others. Because the mount of Venus represents capacity for love, affection, sensuality, desire, and romance, it is the most popular area for palm readers to scrutinize for clues about a person's love life. The mount of Venus also represents home, family, and morality, as well as passionate emotion and physical energy. The mount of Venus relates to drive and zest for life.

PHYSICALITY AND MEANING

If the mount of Venus is overly puffy, it can indicate a fear of commitment and possibly a proclivity for promiscuity. Recognizing the tendencies means the person can make conscious choices for dealing with them.

When the head line and the thumb are both strong and steady, passionate nature is tempered by a sound, moral ability to size up each romantic situation. In that case, the person likely focuses physical passions into material gain, finding success in the boardroom instead of the bedroom.

Of course, love of material pleasures has a price: The person might discover that they are so occupied with creating a wonderful life (with all the material trappings of success) that they don't have the time or inclination for small romantic gestures. If that's the case, the person will have to work harder at balancing material and physical pleasures.

If there is not a well-developed head line or thumb configuration, an exaggerated mount of Venus can indicate a callous, uncaring penchant for instant gratification.

MOUNT OF VENUS PERSONALITY TYPE

Venus represents the forces of love, peace, and beautiful aesthetics. Generally, people with a predominant mount of Venus fall into a physical type with round faces dominated by large doe-eyes and voluptuous lips, while other facial features tend to be smaller than average. These doe-eyed individuals usually stand slightly taller than other types and most often have a very robust, healthy outlook on life. Venusians are the most sensual and socially outgoing of the mount types. They know how to live and love with great passion.

A predominate mount of Venus suggests that the person loves the finer things in life, from luxury items to special works of art. Understanding of emotion indicates that the person would likely excel working in education, politics, or psychology.

A nearly smooth, flat Venus mount can indicate a calculating and overly critical disposition. The person tends to be a kind-hearted lover rather than overtly passionate. The best match for a romantic partner would be someone whose mount of Venus is similar. If a person has a flat Venus mount and can find a partner with a similar structure, there's a good chance for lasting love because neither sees physical passion as a requirement of the relationship.

—— ✦ *Magical Musings* ✦ ——

If you are of the Venusian personality, you may consider working with the Roman goddess Venus or the Greek Aphrodite as your personal deity in meditation or spellwork. You will find that you have a lot in common with these goddesses.

Mounts of Mars

There are two mounts associated with Mars, the planet of action, notable for the energies of aggression and courage. The

Upper Mars mount is located on the outside area of the palm, under the little finger. The mount of Lower Mars is found in the area between the thumb and index finger. These mounts indicate whether or not a person's primary response to challenging situations is to fight or flee (in other words, show courage or seek safety).

Lower Mars shows capacity for physical strength or endurance, while Upper Mars indicates moral values. The mounts of Upper and Lower Mars are sometimes referred to as the mount of Mars Positive (Upper) and mount of Mars Negative (Lower).

UPPER MARS PHYSICALITY AND MEANING

A well-developed mount of Upper Mars indicates that a person is somewhat confrontational, which can be a positive attribute in a crisis. An overdeveloped mount of Upper Mars can mean that a person is a bit of a bully, someone who uses physical force or coercion to get a point across. The overdeveloped mount of Upper Mars indicates that a person is especially competitive when playing games or participating in sports. The person might want to consider balancing the competitiveness with meditation or yoga and should remember to temper their language, as well.

A smooth, flat, or otherwise undeveloped Upper Mars mount reveals that a person dislikes confrontation and seeks to escape stressful situations. However, since the person's strategic and survival skills are superior, he or she excels at defending others and would make a top-notch defense attorney. Fighting injustice suits this personality and mount type well.

A weak or flat mount of Upper Mars suggests the person likely has a difficult time standing up for their rights; however, a well-developed mount indicates they are always ready to take on other people's causes and battles.

LOWER MARS PHYSICALITY AND MEANING

If the mount of Lower Mars is not well developed, the person likely has a fear of confrontation and lack of courage. Despite how that sounds, it's not necessarily a bad thing—it might make the person much more cautious than necessary in certain situations and definitely less assertive. When the Lower Mars mount is overdeveloped, the person may have an overly confrontational, even combative, personality. Ideally, the mount of Lower Mars is well developed and more evenly balanced than these two extremes.

When the two mounts of Mars are developed to the same degree, rising to the same level from the palm, the person's personality is well balanced. Otherwise, the person either possesses tremendous courage and conviction but isn't motivated to use them in a positive direction or they have the energy to act but little conviction or belief, thus unable to decide how to proceed.

MOUNT OF MARS PERSONALITY TYPE

In general, if the palm sports a predominant mount of Mars (whether Upper or Lower), the person has a forceful personality that can easily dominate heated discussion or debate. But the person is also intelligent, social, and fun loving—especially enjoying lengthy discussions about any hot topic of the day. They excel in business and commerce; however, they need to have a predominant Upper Mars mount (rather than a Lower Mars mount) to have an easier time climbing the ladder to success. Physically, Martians are distinguished by their long, angular bone structure, combined with a large mouth and a beak-like nose set between strong cheekbones.

Plain of Mars

Located between the two Mars mounts, in the middle of the nine palm and finger mounts, in the very center of the palm, you will find the plain of Mars. Run your finger along this section of the palm and notice whether the flesh feels thick; if so, it suggests a hot temper. Alternatively, a hollowness of this area reveals that the person might have trouble communicating with others. If the plain of Mars is neither thick nor hollow, the person maintains control and balance of emotions and tends to see things clearly.

Mount of Luna

Find the mount of Luna located next to the percussion area (base of the hand) and opposite the thumb and mount of Venus. This palm area relates to imagination, intuition, and creativity.

When this area is normally developed (neither flat nor too fleshy), the person possesses a creative imagination and a passion for nature, travel, poetry, art, and literature.

If the mount of Luna is overdeveloped, the person might have some difficulty in dealing with reality because imagination gets in the way. Look at the head line to determine whether it is strong enough to handle a vivid and active imagination. Can it ground the person enough so they can clearly assess situations? Or is the head line too weak (faint) to have any equalizing effect?

If the Luna mount is underdeveloped, the person tends to process every new experience purely from a sensual, feeling standpoint—eschewing logic and decisiveness. The ideal Luna mount is of average development, indicative of a healthy balance of imagination and reality.

If the mount of Luna increases in size toward the wrist area (as opposed to near the thumb), the person possesses a strong intuitive sense, seeing beyond physical reality. The person seems to know things before they happen and is adept at planning life accordingly.

✦ *Magical Musings* ✦

Many witches have prominent mounts of Luna because of their advanced psychic abilities. These mounts may not be present at birth but grow over time as a witch develops and hones their craft. Observe yours over time and see if it changes.

MOUNT OF LUNA PERSONALITY TYPE

In general, people with strong Luna mounts on their hands are dreamy, imaginative, creative, and giving. They are very compassionate and helpful to others; often, they are protective of the people they care about. If a personality fits with the mount of Luna type, the person loves to share their creative gifts as writer, painter, or public speaker. They would make a terrific psychic, artist, writer, or composer. If a large Luna mount is coupled with a prominent Venus mount, the person is destined for world renown and acclaim.

A predominant Luna mount in a hand suggests that the person loves water and anything associated with it. They may even live near the ocean or frequently travel there.

If the mount of Luna is not well developed or is smooth or unnoticeable, the person prefers to stay near home and has a tendency to live in their own little shell. If they have any imagination, it's a secret that only their private journal will reveal.

Other Palm Mount Markings

Mounts of the palm, like clouds, suggest shapes (for example, squares, triangles, circles, crosses, and grilles), but the shapes aren't usually exact in their renderings or proportions. Although these shapes can form all over the palm, it's important to note that, on the mounts of the palm, the shapes or markings have distinctly different meanings.

There are five main markings that typically occur on the mounts of the palm. Generally speaking, crosses and grilles represent negative signs, while stars can indicate good luck (especially with money) and squares lessen the impact of negative signs. Mounts containing a triangle indicate wisdom.

✦ Magical Musings ✦

The planetary characteristics in palmistry are very similar to those of astrology. Venus usually tells you about love, and Saturn is normally an old grouch. Once you learn the basics, you can apply them to all forms of divination and spellwork.

Grilles on Venus

Most often, grilles that appear on this mount represent lots of misguided or splintering energy. Is the person passionate about too many things? Grilles warn that too many passions can lead to stress, tension, and an unhealthy intensity of emotions. Balance this intense energy with peaceful and restorative walks, meditation, or prayer.

Stars and Crosses on the Luna Mount

Stars and crosses on the mount of Luna are warnings to be extra diligent when traveling. If the star or cross on the Luna mount is encased in a protective square marking, then the person can safely let their guard down.

Other Markings on the Mars Mounts

A cross on the mount of Lower Mars is common and symbolizes possible harm directed at the person by enemies. Their intention might be to undermine credibility or perhaps something more drastic. Regardless, caution is recommended.

Alternatively, if the palm has the lucky triangle on the mount of Upper Mars, the person will be able to outwit any potential adversary because they are able to identify and work around negative energy. Military or political strategists, as well as athletes and salespeople, frequently are born with this marking.

On the plain of Mars, the most common symbol is the cross. Look carefully at the plain because it is easy to miss symbols that might be present because many lines shoot out in all directions.

A cross in this area of the hand means that the person is likely interested in studies such as alternative medicine, spirituality, and the occult.

Each cross, star, or square will tell you something about an area of the person's life that they need to know more about. For example, the cross sign indicates accidents. If it appears on the mount of Lower Mars, it suggests the possibility of an accidental death, such as in a car crash, but a cross on the mount of Luna could signify widowhood.

FINGER MOUNTS AND MEANING

The finger mounts lie on the palm at the base of each finger area and incorporate the lowest part of the finger. These mounts indicate interests, talents, and skills. Also, when reading the fingers, look for their characteristics and shapes, the spaces between fingers, the length of the fingers, and the relationship of the fingers to the palm.

The mount of each finger is known by the same name as the finger to which it belongs. Also, the mount is ruled by the same mythical god associated with the finger—Jupiter (first finger, closest to the thumb), Saturn (second, middle finger), Apollo (third, ring finger), and Mercury (fourth, pinkie). Thus, in interpretation, each mount shares the same qualities as the finger of which it is a part.

MOUNT OF JUPITER (FIRST FINGER)

The area below the first finger, or forefinger, also known as the Jupiter finger, is called the Jupiter mount. It indicates the person's public persona (aspects they reveal to the world), as well as idealism, honor, courage, and boldness.

A well-developed mount of Jupiter suggests the person is optimistic and has an innate sense of justice; however, a mount that rises higher than the other finger mounts means they desire to control and dominate others and might have a tendency to be arrogant and possibly greedy. A flat, low mount suggests lack of ambition, scattered leadership energies and focus, and a generally weaker personality type.

MOUNT OF SATURN (SECOND FINGER)

The Saturn mount is located underneath the second, or middle, finger. If a predominant mount, the person may already know Saturn's gloomy influence, which can make them conservative, distrustful, and unyielding. A large fleshy mount of Saturn engenders solitary, introverted, and aloof behavior—but the person might be pensive and introspective, as well as cynical and untrusting.

A level mount of Saturn offers a better prognosis. The person is friendly and optimistic. Independent enough to think for oneself, the person balances the polarities of trust and suspicion, new ideas and old values, and the love of solitude and the love of friends. If the person has a midsized mount of Saturn, they exhibit just the right amount of common sense and responsibility. They are not excessive, obsessive, or moody. The person is a leader, capable of bringing leadership qualities into any organization.

If the mount of Saturn is flat, hollow, and otherwise weak, the person may be flighty, irresponsible, and disorganized.

MOUNT OF APOLLO (THIRD FINGER)

The Apollo mount, located at the base of the ring finger, rules the attributes given to Apollo, Roman god of the Sun, who represents light and truth, poetry and art, and healing and beauty.

A raised Apollo mount suggests that the person is outgoing, enthusiastic, talented, creative, lively, and positive. They possess versatility, logic, and understanding and like to lead others, which may at times make them unpopular. Their love for beauty, creativity, and self-expression may also be seen in their skills in crafts, cooking, and fashion, if not in the high arts, or at least in a deep interest in aesthetic subjects.

An extreme mount of Apollo brings out negative characteristics. The person can become opinionated and ostentatious, too easily impressed by power, position, and fame.

If the mount appears flat or hollow, the person will shun the spotlight, cling to their clique, and be willing to settle for a lackluster life; or, they may lack energy due to illness. A weak mount of Apollo makes a person more secretive.

MOUNT OF MERCURY (FOURTH FINGER)

The mount at the base of the pinkie takes its name from the winged-foot messenger god of the ancient Romans. Because the god Mercury ruled over commerce and business, the Mercury mount represents ability to express and communicate ideas. A raised mount indicates interests in travel, business, teaching, and practical matters. A prominent mount of Mercury also reveals aptitude for science and the healing arts, as well as meaningful relationships with friends and children.

A well-defined mount of Mercury suggests many interests and a confident, quick-witted, and excellent communicator.

When action is needed, the person takes charge, whether attending to an emergency or closing a deal. They find it easy to read others.

If the Mercury finger mount is excessively large, the person tends to be chatty or gossipy, possibly embellishing the truth. Regardless, they will use their skillful communication to advance in life.

A flat mount indicates a quiet, shy individual, unable to quickly assess what is going on around them. Or, they might be preoccupied with their own life, with little interest in the lives of others. Also, they might find it difficult to communicate with their partner.

If the Mercury mount veers toward Apollo, there's a good chance that the person is an astute artist who understands the business side of art. They would excel at owning a gallery. They enjoy the little rituals of life and have an innate curiosity and varied interests.

A mount of Mercury that veers toward the edge of the hand, however, suggests that the person is fast thinking, fast talking, fast acting, changeable, and totally absorbed in what they do.

✦ *Magical Musings* ✦

Four or more vertical lines on the mount of Mercury could indicate a propensity for healing. Witches of the past were known as great healers and were sometimes persecuted because their knowledge of herbcraft seemed mystical and foreign.

The Story of the Fingers

Fingers in palmistry are known by their individual, more esoteric names, which correspond with the gods of Roman mythology for the attributes of those divine beings.

Jupiter Leads the Way

The Jupiter (index) finger describes leadership abilities and assertiveness.

If the Jupiter finger extends from the palm out to end at the base of the nail of the neighboring Saturn finger, the person is someone who loves power and desires to lead others. If the finger of Jupiter is as long as the finger of Saturn, egotism shows; the person may even feel the need to control others. A crooked or bent Jupiter finger reveals a tendency to dominate other people, while a short Jupiter finger indicates an aversion to personal responsibility.

Saturn Holds the Secrets of Dark Moods

The Saturn finger is the middle finger; it describes moods as well as responsibilities. A Saturn finger that's noticeably longer than the others connotes a tendency for depression. A shorter than normal Saturn finger indicates a tendency to fear responsibility and pressure, whereas a crooked or bent finger suggests a chip on the shoulder. This is the finger where palmists look for indications of a persecution complex.

Apollo Proclaims Fame

Fame and happiness could be within reach. Take a look at the ring (Apollo) finger, as it reveals the potential to achieve those things. It also suggests interest in the arts or sciences. A long Apollo finger reveals desire to be a celebrity in the creative arts; if the finger is excessively long, however, it indicates a craving for notoriety at any price. A short Apollo finger indicates shunning any kind of notoriety or publicity, preferring instead to keep a low profile, often working behind the scenes. A low-set Apollo finger means that while the person may have an interest in pursuing an artistic career, they may not have been born with the talent to make it happen.

Mercury Balances

Mercury, the fourth finger, points to balance or abuse of power. A long finger means the person might exploit the skills and talents of others for business purposes. If it is extremely long, extending past the base of the nail of Apollo, there's a tendency to be a bit of a fraud. A short Mercury finger means that despite a person's inability to use their own talents to the fullest, they don't like to capitalize on the talents of others. If the Mercury finger is set low, the person is the imaginative, dreamy type. This isn't a bad thing—dreaming begins the process of manifesting; however, when a person dreams but lacks grounding (doesn't set goals or take action) they could face challenges trying to earn a decent living.

Thumbs

The thumb, one of the most important character divulgers on the hand, reveals the fortitude of will and the soundness of judgment. The thumb is an indicator of the degree of self-control and personal willpower, as well as disposition.

Note the length of the thumb. A long, well-formed thumb indicates a strong will and sound judgment. A short, thick thumb means the person can be quite contrary or stubborn.

People with supple-jointed thumbs tend to be reasonable and adaptable and are generally more tolerant, open, and giving than those with firm-jointed thumbs. Such thumbs connote compassion and empathy; these people give their thoughts, time, and cash more freely to the needy. More concerned with intention rather than hard-and-fast rules, they lobby for change for causes they strongly support.

One specific type of thumb is not better or worse than any other. The thumb's shape can give information about potential for ambition and talent, but the person should remember that they can overcome any limitations they have inherited in this life.

Does the thumb appear to have a waistline? Such a thumb looks as though it has a waist, formed by the narrow joint that connects the second phalange to the top of the thumb. This type of thumb represents unwavering tact and the ability to understand lots of different viewpoints. These people's empathy enhances their ability to relate well to others. They probably volunteer and support others, and their empathy is nothing short of profound. Their creative and practical aspects are perfectly balanced.

Reading Wrist Lines

The wrist lines loop around the bottom of the wrist like bracelets and mark the entryway to the hand, the place where the skin patterns begin and the reading of the palm can commence. Traditionally, wrist lines were thought to be an indication of longevity, but there are many other pieces of information that they can tell the palm reader.

Each person in the world has some form of wrist lines, and they are considered one of the nine sets of minor lines that contribute extra interpretive information to a hand. The wrist lines are known as rascettes, and there are generally three of them (though in some cases there may be four). They are sometimes called the bracelets of life because, in the Eastern tradition of palmistry, they are used to determine whether the owner of the hands will have a long life. Each of the lines of the wrist is thought to represent about twenty-five to twenty-eight years of life, so three complete and clear lines represent a substantially long life.

Evaluate Health and Vitality

A clear and deep first rascette line shows that the person is in good health and physically fit. If the first line is poorly formed and unclear, it means that they are indulgent and reckless, and that their problems may be more of their own making than they admit.

If the first wrist line curves upward into the bottom of the palm or is broken up to a large extent, it can mean gynecological troubles for females, from infertility or menstrual problems to difficulty giving birth. In males, it signals urinary, prostate, hormonal, or reproductive problems. Remember to also consider the life line when evaluating what you notice on the wrist lines.

Read Life Length and Quality in the Wrist Line

The first rascette (the one closest to the palm) indicates the quality of the first two to three decades of life, the second the next few decades, and so on. Other palm readers assert that the length of line indicates the length of life, so if that first line stretches across the entire wrist, it means a lifespan of about twenty-five years of good life. Additional lines add to that length.

Although the wrist lines are read as an indication of longevity, they can also reveal other information, such as the inclination to travel. The travel lines that often appear on the Luna mount actually begin on a rascette. There are three things to keep in mind when reading the rascettes for travel:

1. The lines don't extend toward the Luna mount but rather move upward.
2. The length of the travel line will tell you how long the journey will be and how far the person will go.
3. The straighter the wrist lines, the safer the passage on journeys through life will be.

Look for Markings of Good Fortune or Trouble

The lines of the wrist can have various types of markings—crosses, chains, breaks, stars, and so forth. When you are examining the rascettes, don't read further than where the wrist bones meet the radius bone on the arm. When reading rascettes, you always want to stay focused on the major lines around the wrist.

✦ A chain around the wrist symbolizes a life of struggle and hard labor. However, the effort will eventually result in monetary gain.

✦ A star on the first line of the wrist in the midsection of the line means that the person will inherit money early in life.

✦ A cross on a wrist line means that the person will have trouble early in young adulthood when they set out on their own. Immediate family may intrude on their independence, keeping them from growing into their own person.

+ A break in any one of the rascette lines shows an untrustworthy and self-centered aspect. A lack of control over the person's own behavior could mean their downfall.

+ If a rascette is crossed by an angle, the person will be rewarded near the end of life by financial or career advancement.

+ A rascette with a triangle brings good luck, financial gain, honor, and prestige.

Derive Meaning from Wrist-to-Finger Lines

The lines that extend from the wrist to the base of the fingers have meanings that relate to fortune, fame, and travel, with specific interpretations based on the general symbolism of the finger.

+ **Rascette line to Apollo.** A line that travels upward from the rascette to below the Apollo finger means a trip will be a success and lead to honor, renown, and wealth. The trip could even lead to fame that continues after they return home.

+ **Rascette line to Mercury.** A line from the rascette to the Mercury mount will result in a fortune granted in an unexpected manner as a result of a trip.

+ **Rascette line to Saturn.** A line that extends from the rascette to the Saturn mount indicates a trip has trouble and could end in catastrophe.

Notice Marriage Indicators in the Rascettes

If the person is interested in prospects for marriage in their future, look at the lines that rise from the rascettes:

✦ A branch to the Jupiter mount on the hands is a sign that the person will marry into wealth and power.

✦ A branch to Saturn would mean marriage to an older person.

✦ A line that extends from a rascette to the Apollo mount represents a marriage to a person with creative talents and artistic tastes.

✦ Finally, a line to the Mercury mount means a union with a businessperson or merchant, or a marriage as a result of commercial activity (for instance, to someone the person met on a business trip).

✦ Magical Musings ✦

The secret to palm reading, like most forms of divination, is to use your intuition to combine all the bits and pieces and reveal a full picture. Learning the basics will get you started, but once you have them, let your intuition take over.

⟫ FINDING A LOVE MATCH ⟪
THROUGH THE HANDS

If you want an instant take on the personality of a potential lover, take a look at the lines, mounts on the hand, and the fingers. The major lines of the palm—head, heart, life, fate, health, and creativity—all reveal something about relationships. For example, the deep, long furrows in the marriage line on both palms suggest that the people are meant for each other, or at least they are destined to share a bond that will endure. Of course, as you have now learned, if the line is broken, it indicates separation or divorce.

The fate line is a key place to look when you want to learn more about the companions that life will offer. A line of influence or attachment can arise from the mount of Luna to join the fate line—an excellent indicator for a marriage. The lower that the line of influence joins the fate line, the earlier the relationship will be formed.

SPELLBINDING SEX

There's sex…and then there's sensual, passionate, romantic sex. Take a look at your palm's mount of Venus. If it's overly puffy, it can indicate a penchant for promiscuity. People with the personality of a Venus mount type are the most sensual and socially outgoing of them all. They know how to live passionately—and well. The mount of Venus represents love, home, family, sensuality, and morality, as well as passionate emotion and physical energy. This is a good area to check out in the hands of your new interest.

Also take a look at their heart line. In your own palm, if the heart line is heavier than the head line you will likely overrule your head to act upon your need for passion.

Don't overlook the shape of the hands when sizing up a potential bedroom partner. You can't go wrong with the square or earth hand, as they tend to have a healthy libido and are warm and passionate, with a zest for life. Equally important, this lover is emotionally healthy. Even better is if the life line sweeps across the palm in a way that gives lots of room for a large mount of Venus (more than a third of the palm) and the presence of the girdle of Venus (the circle between the bases of Jupiter and Mercury); this represents an exuberant and exhaustive amount of energy to be used in sizzling sex.

USING PALMISTRY FOR LOVE

You truly hold your destiny in your hands. Through free choice and the information you can learn from the lines and patterns on your hands, you alone decide how to manifest your fabulous future. Knowing who you are is the first step to finding the partner of your dreams, and palmistry is just one avenue you can use to accomplish this.

Study the lines on your hands, learn the mounts and the ridges, and then when you meet that romantic interest, take a look at their palms and learn what lies beneath the surface. Use your intuition to determine if you've found a solid match—or if you should keep looking.

— *Chapter 3* —

ASTROLOGY:

YOUR MAGICAL HOROSCOPE FOR LOVE

A strology is a way of looking at the world that many modern witches use to decode and understand the people around them. Witches have found many different ways to utilize this tool, from understanding what energies are going to be present in the coming days to figuring out whether a person could be a soul mate. Although you do not need to be a professional astrologer to be a witch, learning the basics of astrology is helpful in every aspect of witchcraft.

The witches' holidays, called the Sabbats, are based on where the Sun is positioned in the sky, while the esbats (monthly celebrations) focus on the Moon's position. Knowing the basic zodiac characteristics and the current location of the Sun and the Moon is useful in understanding the purpose behind these celebrations and planning rituals. In the pages that follow, you will gain a quick understanding of the basics of astrology and how it applies to finding a partner for life. With just your and your partner's birthdates, you will be able to learn if your personalities are likely to mesh well in life—and between the sheets.

EVERYDAY ASTROLOGY

Astrology has a long history. In the past, it was considered a science that was the backbone of many cultures, and even a tool for advising kings on things like the right time to start growing crops or when to go to war. During ancient Greek and Roman times, the knowledge spread and was then used as a tool for the mágos and the goēs (magician/sorcerer) to look into their own lives. Today astrology is a powerful tool in your witch's toolbox, providing guidance about your work, your love life, and anything else—just as it did for the ancient kings.

Astrology is based on the belief that the positions of the Sun, Moon, and planets at the time of your birth impact your life through energy shifts that mold your personality, influence your romantic relationships, and forecast your future.

✦ Magical Musings ✦

Witches are known for their love of divination, using supernatural means to predict the future and answer questions. Horary astrology is the use of astrology as a form of divination. An astrological chart is cast for the moment a question is asked. Looking at this chart will provide the answer.

Astrology can tell you a lot about a potential partner using just their birthdate, the exact time of their birth, and the location where they were born. But don't worry if you don't have all that information—knowing just the day they were born will give you plenty of information to get started.

If you have all the relevant information, you can enter it into one of many astrology websites and get a natal chart, a document that shows where each planet was located in the sky at the moment of an individual's birth. Using this natal chart and research that has been done over the last millennia, you can start to decode what each planet position means to come up with a unique personality profile.

GETTING STARTED

An easy way to get started in astrology is to focus on just the planet and the sign the person's birth is in, meaning which constellation a planet was traveling through at the moment of birth. Each planet has its own functions, and the astrological signs add qualities and energies. This combination gives you a broader picture of the person. For example, Mars is a planet that shows us how we exert energy and how the body expresses itself. If Mars was located in the constellation Aries at the moment an individual was born, that person's physical body would embody the characteristics of Aries. For example, they may be full of fiery competitive energy and like to participate in sports. They may find it hard to stay seated for too long and always want to be on the go and doing something. Do you know someone like this? You might want to check if their Mars is in Aries.

In this book, we are going to focus on your and your potential romantic partner's Sun signs. The Sun is a major player in most individuals' astrological charts. It generally represents the self and the ego. Figuring out if your Sun sign clashes or connects with another's will give you some quick information about whether or not an upcoming date has serious potential.

SIGNS AND SYMBOLS

Astrology uses glyphs, or symbols, to refer to planets and signs. Don't worry if you have to refer back to what each one means at first. You'll get the hang of it very quickly. Plus, you can use these symbols in spells and on talismans, so they can have multiple uses!

— ✦ *Magical Musings* ✦ —

The glyphs (symbols) for each sign and planet are great to use in candle magic. You can carve the symbol whose energy you would like to invoke into a candle to imbue the essence of the sign into the spell. It's a simple way to add extra energetic influence to your recipe!

Following, you will find the common glyphs for each sign. Remember, signs are the constellations that planets are in, which give them their characteristics. You can use the energy of these signs to tell you general personality information about yourself and your love interest.

THE SUN SIGNS, EXPLAINED

The twelve Sun signs are divided roughly by months, but because those divisions don't follow the months exactly, you may have been born on the cusp between two signs. If you were, then read the interpretations for both signs. Each sign is associated both with a planet and with one of the four natural elements: air, earth, fire, and water. These elements provide further clues to the personality traits associated with the signs.

+ **Aries: March 21–April 19, Mars (fire)**—is bold, courageous, and resourceful. Arian individuals always seem to know what they believe, what they want from life, and where they're going. They tend to take the lead in relationships, often asking out individuals instead of shying away. They're dynamic and aggressive (sometimes to a fault) in pursuing their goals. Arians sometimes lose interest if they don't see rapid results, but their ambition and drive to succeed usually tempers that tendency. They can be argumentative, lack tact, and have bad tempers. But they are also the hardworking trailblazers, symbolized by the sure-footed ram.

+ **Taurus: April 20–May 20, Venus (earth)**—symbolized by the bull, is patient, determined, and singular in their pursuit of goals. Lacking versatility because of the fixed nature of the sign, they compensate by enduring whatever they have to in order to get what they want. As a result, they often succeed where others fail. Most Taureans like the fine arts and enjoy music (often with a talent for it themselves). They also like working with their hands—gardening, woodworking, and sculpting. It takes a lot to anger a Taurus person, but once you do, clear out. The "bull's rush" can be fierce. Venus rules this sign; therefore, Taurus people are usually sensual and romantic, enjoying fine wine and romantic excursions.

+ **Gemini: May 21–June 20, Mercury (air)**—is the sign of individuals who use their brains to explore and understand their world. Their inquisitiveness compels them to visit foreign countries, particularly if the Sun is in the ninth house, where their need to explore other cultures and traditions ranks high. The Gemini's mind demands one thing and their heart clamors for the opposite, accounting for their frequent moodiness. These individuals are fascinated by relationships and connections among people, places, and objects. Their need to analyze everything can be annoying. When this quality leads Geminis into exploration of psychic and spiritual realms, it grounds them. The heart of a Gemini is won by seduction of the mind.

—✦ *Magical Musings* ✦—

A famous Gemini, Gerald Gardner, is known for bringing witchcraft and the pagan religion into the modern world. Many witches started practicing a form of traditional witchcraft known as Gardnerian Wicca in the twentieth century.

+ **Cancer: June 21–July 22, Moon (water)**—needs roots, a place or even a state of mind they can call their own. They need a safe harbor, a refuge in which to retreat. Imagination, sensitivity, and the nurturing instinct characterize this sign. Cancerians are generally kind people, but when hurt, they can become vindictive and sharp spoken. They forgive easily but rarely forget. Affectionate, passionate, and even possessive, Cancerians may be overprotective as parents and smothering as partners and lovers. Cancerians act and react emotionally in the same way the crab moves—sideways. They avoid confrontations, are reluctant to reveal their real selves, and may hide behind their protective urges, preferring to tend to the needs of others. They have a tendency to spend more time pampering their partner in a relationship and may forget about taking care of their own needs. Cancers are often intuitive and psychic, as experience flows through them emotionally.

✦ **Leo: July 23–August 22, Sun (fire)**—loves being the center of attention. These individuals often surround themselves with admirers. Leos offer generosity, warmth, and compassion to those in their orbit who are loyal. As a fixed sign, Leos stand firm in their belief systems. They are optimistic, honorable, loyal, and ambitious. Leos have an innate dramatic sense, and life is their stage. Their flamboyance and personal magnetism extend to every facet of their lives. They seek to succeed and make an impact in every situation. It is no surprise that the theater and performing arts fall under the rule of Leo. If you want a Leo to adore you, make them the center of your world.

✦ **Virgo: August 23–September 22, Mercury (earth)**—is mentally quick and agile. The popular image of a Virgo as a picky, critical, and compulsively tidy person is misleading. Virgos tend to be detail oriented, but they also delve deeply into subjects they study. They are career-oriented people and seem to be interested in doing their jobs efficiently and well. They're happiest when engaged in something that benefits society at large. Virgos tend to be attracted to people who are intellectually stimulating or eccentric in some way. Their standards are high when it comes to romantic relationships, and unless the mental connection exists, the relationship won't last long. Young adult Virgos (those in their twenties) may fall for those who aren't quite good enough for them (especially people who are too critical or not appreciative—an unhealthy match for the Virgos).

✦ **Libra: September 23-October 22, Venus (air)**—seeks balance and may find it through meditation. Librans come in three distinct types: those who are decisive, those who aren't, and those who seek harmony for its own sake. Librans have an inherent need to act democratically, diplomatically, and fairly. Even though Librans are courteous, amiable people, they are not pushovers. They use diplomacy and intelligence to get what they want. Being a Venusian sign, Libras also enjoy the finer things in life. A romantic poem or a beautiful painting will go far in winning their affection.

✦ **Scorpio: October 23-November 21, Mars and Pluto (water)**—includes people who are intense, passionate, and strong willed. They often impose their will on others. For less evolved Scorpios, this willfulness can manifest negatively as cruelty, sadism, and enmity; in Scorpios who are more highly evolved, their will transforms lives for the better. Like Aries, Scorpios aren't afraid of anything. Their endurance allows them to plow ahead and overcome opposition. Individuals of this sign don't know the meaning of indifference. You're either a friend or an enemy—no in-betweens for this sign. As such, relationships with a Scorpio can be very passionate and intense, going from enemies to lovers seemingly overnight. A Scorpio is loyal unless you hurt them or someone they love. Then a Scorpio can become vindictive (biting sarcasm is associated with this sign). The more highly evolved people in this sign are often very psychic, with rich inner lives and passionate involvement in metaphysics. Scorpios are excellent workers: industrious and relentless, excelling at types of work associated with the eighth house—trusts and inheritances, mortuaries, psychological counseling, and the occult.

✦ **Sagittarius: November 22–December 21, Jupiter (fire)**— seeks the truth, expresses it as they see it, and doesn't care if anyone else agrees with them. Sagittarians see the large picture of any issue and can't be bothered with the mundane details. They are always outspoken and can't understand why other people aren't as candid. After all, what is there to hide? Logic reigns supreme in this sign. But the mentality differs from Gemini, the polar opposite of Sagittarius, in several important ways. A Gemini is concerned with the here and now; they need to know how and why things and relationships work in their life. A Sagittarius focuses on the future and on the larger family of humanity. Despite the Sagittarian's propensity for logic, they are often quite prescient, with an uncanny ability to glimpse the future. Sagittarians love their freedom and chafe at restrictions—pinning down a Sagittarian into a monogamous relationship can be difficult at times. Their versatility and natural optimism win them many friends, but only a few ever really know the heart of the Sagittarian.

✦ **Capricorn: December 22–January 19, Saturn (earth)**—is serious-minded, aloof, and in tight control of their emotions. In relationships, it may be difficult to tell if a Capricorn is really that interested in you. Even as youngsters, Capricorns exhibit a mature air, as if they were born with a profound core. Capricorns' slow, steady rise through the world resonates with the image of the goat—their sign's symbol. Easily impressed by trappings of success, they are more interested in the power that wealth represents than money itself. They feel the need to rule whatever kingdom they occupy, whether it is their home, workplace, or business. Although Capricorns prize power and mastery over others, they tend to be subtle about it. Capricorns are industrious, efficient, and disciplined workers. Their innate common sense gives them the ability to plan ahead and to work out practical ways of approaching goals, so they often succeed in their endeavors. Capricorns possess a quiet dignity but have a tendency to worry.

+ **Aquarius: January 20–February 18, Saturn and Uranus (air)**—is an original thinker, often eccentric, who prizes individuality and freedom above all else. The tribal mentality goes against the grain of Aquarians. They chafe at the restrictions placed upon them by society and seek to follow their own paths. Aquarius is the sign of true genius; these people generally have the ability to think in unique ways. Once they make up their minds about something, nothing can convince them to think otherwise. This stubbornness is a double-edged sword; it can sustain them or destroy them. Even though compassion is a hallmark of this Sun sign, Aquarians usually don't become emotionally involved with the causes they promote. In relationships they can seem rather aloof and do not show their emotions easily. Their compassion, while genuine, rises from the intellect rather than the heart.

+ **Pisces: February 19–March 20, Jupiter and Neptune (water)**—needs to explore the world through the emotions.

They can easily become a kind of psychic sponge, absorbing the emotions of people around them. People born under this sign usually have wonderful imaginations and great creative resources. They gravitate toward the arts, specifically to theater and film. Because they are so attuned to the thoughts of people around them, they excel as managers and administrators. There is no one like Pisces to give you good advice. Pisces, though, will put the idea into your head and let you come up with the solution. At times, though, Pisceans can be ambivalent and indecisive because they're so impressionable. In highly evolved types, mystical tendencies are well developed, and the individuals possess deep spiritual connections. Pisces people need time alone to center themselves. Their moods range from joyful, giddy heights to the depths of despair. Love and romance fulfill Pisces emotionally, and they generally flourish within stable relationships.

— ✦ *Magical Musings* ✦ —

Witches live by the power of the Moon and may relate more to their Moon signs than their Sun signs, especially if they were born at night. If the description of your Sun sign doesn't seem to fit you, find out what sign your Moon was in at the time of your birth. To know your Moon sign, your time of birth is important, as the Moon changes signs every two and a half days.

Understanding Houses and House Cusps

Once you understand the roles planets and signs play in astrology, your next step is to look at which house the planet is located in. Houses represent the area that the planet will have the most influence on in the individual's life.

Think of the sky as a circle. Now divide that space into twelve parts. Each part is a house. With the Earth's rotation during the span of a year, the Sun transits from one house to the next.

The division between one house and another is called the cusp. For example, if you have Taurus rising—on the cusp of the first house—then Gemini sits on the cusp of your second house, Cancer on the cusp of the third, and so on around the horoscope circle.

Those who were born at the edge of a house—on days when the Sun was transiting from one house to another—are considered to have been born "on the cusp" and may show traits from the two signs they border. For instance, if you were born on April 19, the cutoff date for Aries, you should also read the interpretation for Taurus for magical insight, because some of those attributes probably apply to you.

Using Astrology to Find Love

Now that you know the basics of astrology, it's time to use intuition to bring clarity to your relationships. Intuition is the essential connection that links the various astrological pieces into a coherent whole, a living story. Take each piece of information you learn and let your gut and instincts discern how they best connect to you. Choosing to align specific areas of your love life in harmony with the energies of the planets gives you the power to make wiser choices about who you date.

Magical Matches

Comparing your Sun sign with that of another person will give you a basic idea of whether or not you'll get along, but this kind of simple observation lacks the depth and breadth that a comparison of natal horoscopes would provide. However, it is a fun and quick way to figure out how compatible you may be without having to dig up the time and location of each of your births.

You can also take a look at the general characteristics of each sign to see how well they blend together. Each sign of the zodiac is associated with one of the four elements (fire, water, air, or earth) and one of the three qualities (cardinal, fixed, or mutable). The combination of the element with the quality creates the backbone of the unique attributes of each zodiac sign.

ELEMENTS

+ Fire signs form relationships quickly…but they can also become easily bored. They are bold and bright, often the aggressors, and like being in the spotlight—not good for partners who might easily become jealous.

+ Water signs are emotionally intense, often spiritually inclined, and have a mysterious air about them…but they can be moody.

+ Air signs are quick and mentally agile, and they like to stir things up. They're all havoc seekers on some level. Libra does it quietly; Gemini is a drama queen and a gossip; and Aquarius is hard to pin down. They give any relationship that uncertainty factor.

✦ Earth signs can fall hard in romantic relationships. They will struggle and protest along the way. They're ten times more sensitive than people think they are—only because they don't necessarily wear their hearts on their sleeves. When they love, they love truly and deeply.

QUALITIES

✦ Cardinal signs are go-getters and will take the lead in relationships. Sometimes they may come off as a little too forward or pushy—but they know what they want and are willing to take it.

✦ Fixed signs like consistency. Once they are in a relationship, they will likely stay in it until their partner breaks it off. They thrive on stability and routine.

✦ Mutable signs can be hot one minute and cold the next. They are sometimes hard to pin down and will flourish in relationships that are always changing.

♥ ARIES IN LOVE

Aries individuals have a penchant for doing things their way. They're as sharp as tacks, and those with whom they form relationships respect them, though others may think they're bossy and domineering. But they know what they want, and they're perfectionists about it. If you get into a fight with them, be prepared! Aries excel at debating. They like to win every argument—even when they're wrong. And be careful not to get too jealous with an Aries. They hate it. They need to know that they can do whatever they want to do.

More mature Aries, on the other hand, handle people with charm and finesse. They're a lot less aggressive than immature Aries—on the outside—though their thought processes may be very similar. Where the immature Aries drives forward, the mature Aries will pull back and wait for their lover to come to them—and they usually do. When it comes to love, the mature Aries is just as fickle and stubborn as the typical Aries.

With Aries, it may be wise to take everything with a grain of salt. Remember that they're the children of the zodiac, too, and that they'll usually want more of what they cannot truly have. With Aries, you have to change the rules frequently, or they'll get bored.

Aries charm and self-assurance can woo you into bed with well-placed words. Once there, their skill depends on the particular Aries. They are often confident—too confident—in bed. And they are sensitive, too. They might tell you about their own downfalls, but they will freak out if you start listing them.

Aries tend to be a bit selfish in bed, too. Their confidence allows them to know what they want and ask for it, so make sure you stick up for yourself and tell them what you want. They can woo you to the ends of the Earth, but they can also be detached. You'll believe you know them, and then they will change right before your eyes.

Tips

Aries can be incredibly loving and sweet, and they almost always get what they want in love. Their only regret is that someone they love may not be good enough for them, as they perceive it. Most times, once they fall out of love, it's gone forever.

Make Aries work for everything—they would rather see the results of hard work rather than just be handed the prize right out of the gate. Never put them on a pedestal—treat them as an equal. Praise them only when they deserve it. Make them listen to you but understand that they will only see their side of it. Accept this. Don't ever try to control them, or they will run the other way. Give them freedom but also set boundaries.

Matches with Aries

If you want an Aries who lives for love, find an Aries with their Venus in Cancer or Pisces. Aries, because it's a fire sign, is often attracted to other fire signs—Sagittarius or Leo. But generally, unless aspects in the chart indicate otherwise, romance with another fire sign can be explosive. Aries gets along well with air signs—Gemini, Libra, or Aquarius—or a sign that's sextile (60 degrees) or trine (120 degrees) from Aries on the horoscope wheel. Sometimes, an earth sign—Taurus, Virgo, or Capricorn—helps ground all that Aries energy. In chart comparisons, a Venus or Moon in Aries in the other person's chart would indicate compatibility.

✦ Magical Musings ✦ ---

If you want a spell to act fast, add the energy of Aries to the ingredient list. As a cardinal fire sign, Aries energy is quick and bold, sometimes acting rashly. Find a symbol of a ram to add into a sachet or use the word *Aries* in a rhyme to activate this intense energy.

♥ Taurus in Love

In romance with a Taurus, a lot goes on beneath the surface. Taureans are subtle and quiet about what they feel. Once they fall, though, they fall hard. In fact, their inherently fixed natures simply won't allow them to give up. Perhaps this tendency sounds like it could be good for you and bad for them. But sometimes Taurus people get in way over their heads and then find that there's no turning back.

However, a Taurus will never really fall in love unless they think they can trust you. Trust goes a long way with Taurus. Deep down, Taurus knows that they are sensitive and that they take themselves a little too seriously. Their sense of responsibility weighs heavily on their shoulders, and they'll always fulfill any task they believe they must.

But, remember that they will feel like it's up to them to judge the world. If they're critical, take it as a warning. They have an idea of how things should be, and they may try to mold you into how they see you or how they would like to see you. Pay close attention to their naggings because, though it may seem otherwise, they mean every word they say.

Sometimes, it's not clear if a Taurus is in love with you or in love with the *idea* of you. Ego comes into play with a Taurus, and sometimes their win-win attitude will outweigh their real need for you. If you're not sure, trust your gut. Deep down, you'll know the difference.

As a Venus-ruled sign, Taureans are true sensualists and romantic lovers. Their romantic attachments ground and stabilize them. Love is like air to them; they need it to breathe. Again, they'll want to trust and rely on you. This is essential. In fact, it's very easy to see if Taurus trusts you, at least to some degree. Taurus can't touch and make love unless they feel they can. Taurus and Virgo may be the only individuals in the zodiac who are like this. They might entertain a fling or two in their lifetime, but that's not what they're about.

Taurus individuals have a habit of falling for fire signs. In the beginning, the fire sign will conquer them. But once Taureans start getting comfortable, they begin flirting with others and testing them. If they lighten up, they just may be able to keep them.

Taurus individuals are looking for meaning and true love—for someone who'll put up with their obstinate nature and even revel in it. Some Taurus individuals have a lot of bravado. Like the bull, they're quite direct and will usually take a problem head-on (the opposite of the way Cancer would handle it). Give them a good love challenge and they won't shy away. Taurus is built for competition. The problem is they may never really stop to consider if you two are actually good for one another.

Unlike most other signs, don't deal with a Taurean on a physical level after you two argue. You'll probably need to talk things out before you make love again. Remember, Taurus is sensitive and puts their heart into lovemaking. Don't try to make up with them with kisses.

With Taurus individuals, it is better to grapple with issues as they come up—don't go to bed angry. Taurus is good at dealing with the issues at hand. However, if they push them deeper and deeper, you will have a difficult time getting them out again. When you bring it up, they'll look at you like they have no idea what you're talking about—even if they are steaming inside. Instead, they'll talk about it years from now when you least expect it.

In fact, Taurus is capable of holding a grudge for decades. It's very difficult for them to let go of the past.

Try to be direct and honest with Taurus all the time. Don't let them get on a self-pity track; it's their armor. If a partner from their past has wronged them, they'll look for every conceivable indication that you'll do the same to them.

Tips
....

Find out where your Taurus is sensitive and make sure you stay far away from that route. If an ex cheated on them, go out of your way to show them that you're more than trustworthy. If an ex was using them for money (or, more likely, they were simply convinced that they were), make sure they know that you're just the opposite.

Taurus loves all sensual things—including food! And they love domestic prowess. Cook a wonderful dinner for Taurus and you'll get extra points. When they're relaxed, you can give them a massage or touch them in any way—they'll get the hint. They are sensitive with touch as well. Just don't rush things. Make sure they are in love before you go to bed with them. If you don't, they may lose respect for you and think that you do the same with everyone.

Also, a Taurus wants to know that they are truly loved before they'll hit the sack with a partner. They can have flings, but as they get older and get to know themselves better, they'll realize that this is not the best of all possible worlds. They'll want to wait and be romanced. And there's no one who knows how to seduce like Taurus.

Matches with Taurus

Air signs mesh well with earth signs because they're both thinking signs, whereas water and fire signs are more spontaneous and apt to follow their hearts more. Gemini will entertain Taurus, but Taurus won't necessarily trust them. Libra may be a good bet for Taurus, as both have an incredible affinity for an elegant, sumptuous, and refined life. Libra and Taurus manage to acquire it together by spurring each other on. Aquarius's lifestyle will drive conservative Taurus crazy, despite the attraction.

♥ GEMINI IN LOVE

One issue you may run into with Gemini is that they don't really know what they want. They think they know, but then it changes. Gemini individuals need to work for love, and then they'll give their all. Also, they need a partner who makes them laugh—but not about themselves. Geminis can be touchy and sensitive when the humor comes at their expense.

Geminis love first with their minds. Even a relationship that begins primarily because of a sexual attraction won't last if there's no mental connection. Quite often, Geminis first seek friendship with the opposite sex, and then, once a mental rapport is established and they're really ready for something serious, the friendship deepens into love. True, they can be quite fickle in their affections, sometimes carrying on simultaneous relationships. But once their hearts are won, they love deeply.

In the same vein, once Gemini is over you, it's really over. Don't ever "take a break" with Gemini—the relationship won't ever come back around to the way it was. Gemini has this power to cut it off clean and never look back once they've decided it's through.

Geminis have a "need to try everything once" attitude. They're like children who need to stick their hands in the cookie jar. Some Geminis won't sleep with a person if they're not in love, but chances are, they'll try it all with the one they're with at the moment.

Geminis may veer toward being drama queens and kings. They like to entertain people, make others laugh, and give good, grown-up advice (that they only wish they could follow themselves). No one can tell a story like a Gemini. They'll use their eyes and body to create a moment. And they'll get as emotionally worked up the seventh time they tell a tale as they did the first time. Don't ever take the stories at face value, though. Gemini has a habit of exaggerating, even when they don't mean to.

Although Geminis give great advice, they're not always great at taking advice from others. And they change their minds frequently, so it's sometimes difficult for them to get to the heart of the matter. Geminis do love wholeheartedly. Capable of diplomacy, they use it when they feel the need but not when it involves love, romance, and you.

If you have a head for business or simply a good job, this will impress Geminis to the umpteenth degree. They want to respect their partner and know that their partner has big ambitions. Geminis are not wallflowers. They want to brag about what a great person they've got at their side. Geminis like to feel like they've got the prize that other people covet. In other words, it's not just okay that they think you're great; they need to know that their friends think you're amazing, too. So, don't hang on them at parties. Show that you're independent but that you're on their side.

Geminis have a bit of a paranoid, insecure thing. You may not see it right away, but it's there. Never go against Geminis in front of their friends. They'll be instantly offended and look elsewhere for love (with someone who will be faithful in their eyes). You don't have to show them your love and devotion immediately; just make sure you agree with them in front of people they deem important.

Be careful with a Gemini and your heart. In love, they tend to leave a few options open. Boredom, to a Gemini, is death. They need the challenge of tempting and wooing you. Before you get comfy and cozy with a Gemini, make sure they're smitten!

Tips

Geminis need a little drama to know that you're interested, but they don't like being alone for long. They can get caught up with their work for a while, but work will never be the most important thing in life—not deep down. Love is the real focus. In fact, they'll stay with someone they think is the best they can find. And if you stay in their good graces, they'll be with you always.

There's a fine line between making Geminis jealous and making them insane. If you make them jealous in an innocent way—but they still trust you—it's fine. If you truly make them jealous, there's no one more vindictive and crazy than they will be. You won't like this side of them at all. It's not pretty.

Geminis also know that sarcasm and humor with an edge is the best remedy for everything. Make a Gemini laugh and they'll instantly think you're smart. With Geminis, it's not always about book smarts; it's about street smarts and ironic, sarcastic comebacks that are funny, not biting or nasty. Geminis can be sensitive in general, but they love to gossip and to make fun of others.

Matches with Gemini

Geminis are social enough to get along with and be attracted to just about anyone on a superficial basis. They feel most at home with other air signs, particularly Aquarians, whose minds are as quick as theirs. They also get along with Sagittarius, their polar opposite in the zodiac, who share some of the same attributes. Again, though, these are broad generalizations. It's important to compare the individual charts.

When Gemini is ready to settle down, an earth sign may be a good option for a partner. A Virgo will be a bit too critical for the thin-skinned Gemini, but a Taurus, with their feisty sensual side, may just be a solid match. Capricorns can go either way, but most Capricorns won't put up with a Gemini's otherwise flighty antics or superficial skimming of political ideas that hold great truths for Capricorns.

Again, an air sign like Libra may be ideal for Gemini if they can find a balance of minds. If anyone can find that rare balance, it's Libra. The only problem is that Libra despises confrontation and Gemini relishes it. Water signs are probably too sidestepping for feisty Gemini, unless they have a lot of earth or air in their charts. Scorpio and Gemini match up well in bed, but Scorpio sometimes can drag down a Gemini when they want to go out and play. Leo can be a fun dating partner for Gemini—with a lot of laughter—but Leo may get annoyed when Gemini doesn't praise the ground they walk on. If Gemini does, it's a match made in heaven.

♥ CANCER IN LOVE

Cancers can be evasive when it comes to romance. They flirt coyly, yet all the while they're feeling their way through the maze of their own emotions. Cancers feel deeply, but Cancers are also very good at putting their feelings on hold. In other words, if they're not already in love with you, they can pull back and see the relationship for what it is at a distance.

On the one hand, if they're in love, it's not so easy for Cancer to let go. On the other hand, Cancer might just cheat on you rather than confess that they are unhappy in the relationship with you. Cancers excel at dodging questions and confronting important issues. They find it difficult to open up and talk about their true, personal feelings. The whole sidestepping part of Cancer is true. True to their crab sign, they mimic the crustacean with surprising accuracy.

Some Cancers dislike the courtship element of romance altogether and prefer to get right down to the important questions: Are we compatible? Do we love each other? The problem is, they tend to go through this by themselves or with a very close friend—not with you. In this case, you must be direct and ask what's going on.

Cancers are homebodies and enjoy entertaining at home, where they feel most relaxed and secure. They feel comfortable around water, too. From the fluidity and calmness of water spring their vivid imaginations. Cancers are "idea" people and can explain any strange, unusual, or outrageous concept to you.

Just remember, to live with and love a Cancer, you have to accept the intensity of their emotions. It's a war they have within themselves, and they'll want to embroil you in it.

But it's not all seriousness for Cancers; they also like to make fun—and will do it just to get your goat. Play along. If you act too touchy, they'll think you're rigid, and that could trigger one of their many unfathomable moods.

— ✦ *Magical Musings* ✦ —

All witches, especially those born under the influence of the lunar-ruled Cancer, know not to schedule any important meetings or phone calls when the Moon is "void." This means that the Moon is not making any important angles to other planets in the sky. During this time, communication and business issues can go awry and any outcome may not be in your favor.

Tips

Perhaps the worst thing you can do with a Cancer is to take everything too literally. If you don't understand subtleties, forget Cancer. They're good at seeing the big picture. They stall at the idea of future and forever after, but they'll know, deep down, when they get there. One thing is for sure: Cancers aren't always faithful, but once they make a strong commitment, they'll stick to it.

Cancers also like to take care of others. If you are in a relationship with a Cancer and get a cold, make sure to let them know. You may end up with a nice warm bowl of soup at your door. Cancers are the nurturers of the zodiac and love to spread their affections to those they are close to.

Matches with Cancer

On the surface, Pisces, as the other dreamy water sign, would seem to be the most compatible with a Cancer. But Pisces's all-over-the-map style combined with Cancer's sidestepping could be frustrating for both. Plus, the duality of Pisces would, most likely, drive a Cancer person crazy. One of the best combinations here is with water sign Scorpio. Cancer manages Scorpio with bravado and knows how to get the ever-changing Scorpio hooked. A little mystery goes a long way with Scorpio, and, in the case of this match, Cancer cannot help but induce a little intrigue with their bottled-up emotions that just lie beneath the surface. Scorpio might just bring those emotions out of Cancer.

Earth signs—Taurus, Virgo, and Capricorn—are particularly good for Cancers with Taurus and Virgo because they are sextile to Cancer. Fire signs with Cancer, on the other hand, tend to bring out the worst in Cancer. In rare cases, Leos do well with Cancers (especially if the Leo is more masculine).

♥ LEO IN LOVE

Leos are passionate. They can also be impulsive and irrational, but it's all part of the charm. They're fickle, and they like to test their partners before they put their hearts into anything. They can be difficult, too, particularly when their egos need to be stroked. If you treat a Leo with anything but the ultimate respect, they may not say anything, but they'll remember it—and count it against you.

Though Leos give the appearance of being confident and secure, this is often an act. Leo's innermost desire is to be accepted for who they are, and their biggest worry is that people will soon discover they're just normal or boring. It's very important for a Leo to feel special.

Leos fight fiercely, so be sure to stick up for yourself with them. On the other hand, arguing for the sake of arguing will make Leos insane. Leos are intense and will argue, but their sunny, calm natures are truly made for being content and feeling safe and comfortable with a partner.

Tips

Make Leos feel secure and they'll be more likely to fall in love with you. But making them secure doesn't mean making yourself a doormat. Let Leo know they can be themselves with you—that you won't judge them—and they'll relax in your presence and soften their claws. For the most part, Leos need to feel needed and want to know they are loved before they commit entirely. Once they're committed, everything is bigger than life and brighter than the Sun. They're known to be loyal, but this is only true after they've found themselves. If they haven't, and they're not yet emotionally evolved or secure, they can be as two-faced as Gemini can be.

Like all fire signs, Leo needs to respect you in order to fall in love. This means that you need to be ambitious in career, straightforward in your dealings with people, and truthful with them. Anything else will be the end of the relationship.

Leos need to believe that a relationship is their idea. If you push too hard, you may scare them off. They like to win—Leos always like a prize. *You* need to be the prize they win. Leos won't mind putting up a fight for you. There needs to be a fine line, though. If you make Leos work too hard, they'll just walk away. This, for example, isn't true of Aries, another fire sign.

If you're involved with a Leo, make sure you know their intentions with you. Ask them. They'll tell you. Leos are not very good liars. If you ask them in person, chances are that you'll get the truth from them. (Or you'll at least read it in their facial expressions—pay attention.)

— ✦ *Magical Musings* ✦ —

If you are planning a romantic night for your partner, look to when the Moon is in a fire sign (Aries, Leo, or Sagittarius). This will add extra passion and intensity to any romp in the bedroom!

Matches with Leo

Another fire sign is good for a Leo because the energy levels are similar. Any sign that is sextile, an angle of separation of 60 degrees or more between two planets (Gemini, for instance), or that is trine, an angle of separation of 120 degrees between two planets (Aries), would be fine too—though Leo has little patience for Aries who aren't spiritually evolved. True, these signs may win Leo for a while, but then what? Leo can be too headstrong. Aries is a lot like Sagittarius with Leo—lots of fire, but not the same temperament. Sagittarius can be a bit too wise and quiet (or even too superficial or stubborn) for Leo; Aries can be too demanding and controlling.

The polarity between Leo and Aquarius, its polar opposite sign, may elevate a Leo's consciousness to where it succeeds best—to the wider world beyond themselves—if the Leo has some air signs in their chart. Capricorn can be an interesting match, and Scorpio seems like a go until Leo realizes that they may not like the way Scorpio may raise their children. But they're surely a good match in bed.

♥ VIRGO IN LOVE

Virgos tend to be inscrutable in the affairs of the heart. They seem remote and quiet one minute, then open and talkative the next. This is due only to Virgo's battle within themselves. They're sensitive but don't like to show it. Sometimes they'll need to show you how they feel; other times they'll keep their feelings a secret. Unfortunately, they don't always let you see this true side of themselves. They're too busy weighing all the options and trying to act the way they think they should, not how they truly feel.

Virgos like everything perfect: every moment, every deed, and every word. They're idealists, but in a practical way. They believe that everything should fall into place on its own (even if it shows no sign of happening) and tend to stay in relationships much longer than they should because they don't want to give up and walk away. To them, you are the investment of their precious time. They also hold on to the past like Cancers and, unfortunately, apply past experiences to present ones. In a perfect world, this would make sense (to them). Unfortunately, each situation is different, and Virgos must face this fact.

The world is a complicated place, and most of us have skeletons in our closets. But for Virgo, there are too many skeletons. They want perfection (mostly from themselves). They'll generally keep their imperfections in the dark, though they'll be the first to point out some of their more superficial flaws. Pay attention to what Virgos tell you, as it's usually all true.

Virgos are incredibly romantic when they feel it. They have a wonderful appreciation of love—and know how to attract people the right way. They seem more practical than idealistic, but deep down, Virgos suffer for love and feel their emotions intensely.

Virgos try to make everything fit into their idea of a perfect world. For example, they're very serious about the words they and others use. If you tell a Virgo something, they expect you to follow through on your promise. They will put their heart and soul into finding a solution for you. If you don't at least try it their way, they'll seriously discredit you.

Virgos tend to be critical, and they can't help it. Don't take it personally, though. Virgos are never harder on the people they love than they are on themselves. Virgos need to analyze, sort through, and mentally take stock once in a while in order to feel grounded and stable.

Here's the bottom line: If you ask Virgo for advice, you'd better take it or at least make them think you're doing something practical about your situation. Virgos will always tell you what to do and expect you to do it. If you get advice from Virgo and ignore it, they'll be less likely to help you in the future.

Tips

The best way to handle a Virgo's lecturing and criticizing you is to tell them they're right about whatever they are picking at, at least in the moment. Then bring it up later to dispute, if you like. Although Virgos must have a sense that they're right, they're also self-aware. In fact, they'll be the first to admit that they're difficult and hardheaded.

You may have to do some grunt work to get on a Virgo's good side. If you show a Virgo that you're easy to get along with and can take their criticism with a healthy show of acceptance, they'll feel more comfortable with you and will eventually let their guard down completely.

Virgos are conflicted within and, therefore, will come across as being nitpicky or too precise. The truth is they've got thin skins.

Matches with Virgo

Virgos are mentally attracted to Geminis, but they find the twins a bit hard to take for the long run. The dramatic and airy nature of Geminis, too, contrasts with Virgos' obstinate nature.

Gemini likes interesting discussions (as does Virgo) and entertains Virgo well, but Virgo sometimes fights fiercely and Gemini prefers subtle and playful confrontation.

✦ *Magical Musings* ✦

Mabon, or the autumnal equinox, occurs as the Sun moves from Virgo to Libra. Mabon is the second of three harvest festivals celebrated by many witches. It is a time to give thanks for the bounty that the Earth has provided and prepare for the darkness that is heralded by Samhain.

Instead, the grounding present in other earth signs may seem appealing on the surface, but leave it to a Virgo to find fault with their fellow earth signs. Scorpios and Cancers may be the best bets, with mystical Pisces a close second. Libra sometimes goes well with Virgo, but it may seem like Virgo is always just out of reach with a Libra, with Virgo never quite getting all the love and devotion they want as Librans try to be fair and balanced in their dispersal of affections. Libra makes it tough.

Fire signs can be great friends with Virgo, but the two might never truly understand the other's intentions. It depends on the rest of their charts. Virgo can patronize without knowing it, and sensitive fire signs take offense. In the end, anyone with a good heart and a sensitive-but-practical nature will get along well with Virgo.

♥ LIBRA IN LOVE

Libras are drawn to beauty, whatever its form. The only thing they enjoy as much as beauty is harmony. Even when a relationship has gone sour, a Libra hesitates to be the one who ends it. Libras can't stand hurting anyone's feelings; emotional rawness is one of those ugly realities that they don't like to see. As a result, they may remain in a relationship longer than they should because they dread the breakup. Libras seek harmony because, in their hearts, they know that enlightenment lies at the calm center of the storm.

In fact, Libra is just that—the eye of the storm. They'll start something and then walk away to watch things unfold at a distance, where it's safe. Libra is the ultimate watcher of human behavior. They study it—study you—and determine what they know and what they believe from that. They'll have their friends study you and see if you're faithful and worthy. Ultimately, they'll make up their own mind. But if a Libra doesn't trust you, you're history. They'll never put the time in to get to know you.

Libra has a very fixed idea of what they're looking for. If you don't fit that perfect mold, they're not going to waste their time on you. Find out what your Libra wants. If you don't, you may seduce them for one night, but they won't get serious with you.

It seems as if Libras have many friends. True, they have a wonderful social circle and many people who believe in them. But watch closely. Librans keep their true self hidden from the world. There's usually only one person they truly trust, often a family member. If they open up to you completely on a consistent basis, you've got a real mate for life.

In fact, Librans can be very stubborn when deciding what the roads of life all lead to. It's sometimes difficult for them to make a tough decision, but when they do, no one can talk them out of it. Librans believe in signs, red flags, and even superstitions. They'll consider omens and apply them to their own lives.

Also, Librans want to be calm and comfortable in a relationship. Many Librans choose younger partners just to have this feeling of ultimate control. Alternatively, they pick individuals a lot older than they are so the partner does all of the deciding. Whether they are the type that requires control or the individual who wants others to make decisions for them, when they love, they love deeply.

Librans have a tough time figuring out what they really want. On one hand, they want a partner who's carefree and easy to deal with. On the other hand, they want someone who's a true confidant and partner for life. Let them battle it out on their own. If they haven't determined yet what they want, stay away.

Tips

Remember that Libras like to feel in control. In this way, you may have to be demure in the beginning. Let Libras chase you. Don't let their friends know that you're interested. Libras will get the hint just by looking you in the eyes. Their eyes are the key to their soul. In fact, that's how you'll know that a Libra is interested.

Libras are very sensitive, so try not to make the first move. Because of the internal battle all Libras must face, they like to have dominance in the situation, and they tend to judge a mate unfairly if they're too aggressive. Once again, let Librans steer the conversation and the relationship. Pull back, at first, and let them court you. They'll do it in a grand way, and you'll be glad you did.

Matches with Libra

Librans can get along with just about anyone. They are most compatible with other air signs, Aquarius and Gemini. Though seriously outgoing, Geminis can sometimes scare them—they understand the way Librans think. Scorpios get to the heart of the matter with Libras, they have the intensity and emotional depth that Librans crave. In fact, Librans might even get attached to Scorpios in a volatile and unhealthy way if they're not careful. Though Scorpios can be a good match for Libras, they should watch out for signs of control. If Librans feel they're being manipulated in any way, they'll be out the door in a flash.

Librans also gravitate toward people who reflect their refined tastes and aesthetic leanings, like Leo. Also, an earth sign may provide a certain grounding that Libran need. Taurus is a wonderful, sensual match with Libra. A water sign, like Cancer, may offer a fluidity of emotion that a Libran may lack, but this combination may be an uphill battle. Cancers can be too moody, sometimes, and too self-involved for harmony-seeking Librans.

✦ Magical Musings ✦

The eighth house in astrology is the domain of occult activities. If you can get your hands on your complete natal chart, see if there are any planets located in this house. This will tell you any special talents or abilities you may have in witchcraft.

Since opposites attract, Aries can sometimes be a good fit for Librans—though Aries need to have found themselves spiritually before this match can work. A Libra with a Libra can be a good match—but watch out! Two of the same signs together can be wonderful…or a big mess.

♥ Scorpio in Love

You don't know the meaning of the word *intensity* unless you've been involved with a Scorpio. No other sign brings such raw power to life. The rawness probably isn't something you understand or even like very much, but there's no question that it's intricately woven through the fabric of your relationship.

The odd part is that you're never quite sure how the intensity is going to manifest: jealousy, fury, endless questions, or soft and intriguing passion. Sometimes, the intensity doesn't have anything to do with the relationship but with the personal dramas in the Scorpio's life. Many times, you may even hear from their work colleagues that they're a perfectionist, and difficult to work with.

If you're in for the long haul, then accept your Scorpio the way they are. If you're not in for the long haul, why try to make them into something different? In any case, Scorpios are all about transformation—it's just that in their case, it means changing the way others around them see the world.

Scorpios have a legendary magnetism. It doesn't even matter if they're good-looking—the draw is always there. Consider this: Scorpios are always the sexiest people in the room. Astrologers say that Scorpios are also known for their bedroom prowess. Unfortunately, other problems can weigh Scorpio down, so they've got to be clear of mind and calm in order to woo you in their cool, mysterious way.

If your Scorpio is completely direct with you, consider yourself lucky. Chances are they've got a number of secrets they keep hidden from the world. It may be something that's happened in their past, or a fetish they don't want to let you in on, or even another individual they see occasionally.

You'll always be able to tell when Scorpio is fibbing. You can feel it because the energy around them changes. If you keep insisting that they tell you the truth, they may even get angry. If they do, it probably means there's something they're not telling you. The only way to get it out of them is to get them in a good mood and pretend you don't really care. Then coax the confession out of them.

Scorpio's senses are strong, especially those of sight, touch, and taste. If they touch you, you'll feel it down to your toes. However, there's one sense they may not focus on: hearing. It may seem at times as if they don't hear anything you say. It's not that they don't really remember. Instead, they have a mental block against things they don't want to know. Very likely they'll pretend they don't know what you're talking about. Actually, Scorpios have excellent memories so don't let them get away with this.

Many Scorpios are hidden workaholics. They need to complete the task at hand before they can go on to the next. They're very good, in the beginning, at concealing this fact. Therefore, the thing that will be most important for a Scorpio is to get you. Then, predictably, they'll go back to their normal routine of working crazy hours, complaining about it, and never resolving the problem.

Many Scorpios have obsessive tendencies, which you may not see in the beginning. At first it may just seem like you're another obsession. They'll be so bent on getting you that you'll wonder if you've just stepped into a romance novel. Be aware that this may change later. Scorpios can't leave the duties of their job for long—they define themselves by them.

Know, too, that if they're having many problems at work, your relationship will suffer. They need to resolve work issues before they can think of getting intimate again. They cannot separate these two parts of life, try as they do. In this respect, you must understand and be supportive. There's no other way around it.

In the case of Scorpio, before you even think of letting romance get the better of you, ask yourself: Is this person happy with life? Do they pity themselves? If a Scorpio is not happy, deep down, they will go into periods of self-doubt and pity—and will bring you down with them. Some Scorpios are emotionally mature and can handle the world around them. Find out first, though.

✦ Magical Musings ✦

Many stereotypical antihero characters such as Sherlock Holmes, Jay Gatsby, and Don Draper are based on the general habits of Scorpios. At your next coven meeting, why not play an astrological love game? List all the sexy stars you have crushes on and then try to figure out what sign you think they are. After, go online and see how many you got right!

Tips

Typically, Scorpios stay in a romantic situation that's not working for longer than they should. If they start pulling away a little, or are less jealous or possessive than they were before, you're probably losing them. The worst thing that you can do at this point is to chase after them. Let them come after you. Scorpios are lonely, private souls—yet they hate being alone.

If you are looking to discuss something sensitive or important with a Scorpio, try approaching the subject after lovemaking. Their guard will likely be let down almost completely. Be aware of the potential for Scorpio's temper. They like to bottle things up inside and then it all comes out at once—in a huff. It is not wise to try to convince Scorpios they're wrong at this point. Let them calm down first; then they're more likely to see your side of it.

Matches with Scorpio

Scorpio is usually compatible with Taurus, because the signs are polar opposites and balance each other. The water of Scorpio and the earth of Taurus mix well. However, both signs are fixed, which means that in a disagreement neither will give in to the other. Scorpios can be compatible with other Scorpios as long as each person understands the other's intensity and passions. Pisces and Cancer, the other two water signs, may be too weak for Scorpio's intensity, unless a comparison of natal charts indicates otherwise.

Fire signs may blend well with Scorpio, depending on their charts. If a Scorpio is emotionally solid, a Leo may be a good match. Scorpio loves Leo's sunny nature and is drawn to it. If Scorpio doesn't pull Leo down, this can work. Sagittarius, especially if Scorpio is near the cusp of Sagittarius, can be the same. If the two can respect each other and find a good balance, this can be a working partnership. Aries and Scorpio, however, will find that the emotional gap is probably too wide a chasm to cross.

♥ Sagittarius in Love

Sagittarius carries two interesting themes: the individual who searches for truth outside themselves and the individual who finds their truth in another person. No matter whom a Sagittarian loves or marries, there will always be a part of him or her slightly separate and singular. Sagittarians are pretty clear in what they want. They know if they're in love—or not. Enticing a Sagittarius to fall in love with you can be challenging. Playing hard to get might capture their attention, but they will rely on their instincts and intellect to decide if you are the one they want and need…or not.

Sagittarians are not very diplomatic souls. They tend to be blunt and tactless with words that can sometimes cut you to the bone. For better or worse, believe everything that comes out of Sagittarius's mouth. If they tell you they're in love, they are. If they tell you they're not, they're not. In their mind, honesty and straightforwardness are everything, and they like someone who will listen carefully to everything they have to say.

Strangely enough, Sagittarians sometimes give the impression that they're lost in another world. They seem quiet—or into themselves. This isn't entirely true. In truth, they're probably thinking about work or some problem in quantum physics—they're not likely thinking about your relationship unless it presents a problem for them to solve.

Sagittarians want everything to go smoothly. In their mind, if things are not moving forward, they're not going to waste their precious time on you. Just don't badger them for their thoughts.

Tips

Let Sagittarians come to you to ask how you're feeling. They need to be left alone to experience their space and freedom, and then they'll come search you out.

Sagittarians like to think about big-picture issues, like why we are here, what the purpose of life is, and what the ultimate sacrifice is that a human can make. Instead of making your relationship a challenge for them to untangle, your time would be better spent telling them your own ideas about these major life questions.

The typical Sagittarian loves adventure. They prefer exploring the pyramids of Egypt or learning about an ancient world to sitting on a beach sipping a fruity cocktail. If this sounds like your idea of fun, finding yourself a Sagittarian may add great excitement to your life.

Matches with Sagittarius

Air signs are compatible with Sagittarius. The Sagittarius-Gemini polarity confers a natural affinity between the two signs. But other fire signs might work well, too. It just depends. Sagittarius, above all other fire signs, is the most emotionally secure. Sagittarians are not the most stable (Leos are), but they *think* they are. This can make them a bit of a know-it-all. They don't tolerate as much as Leo, but they're not as ridiculously immature as Aries can sometimes be.

The best match for Sagittarius is a water sign, particularly Pisces. These two go together so well because Pisces is strong and sensual enough for Sagittarius and also a master in the art of silent persuasion. A water sign might do them good because they like being shown the way; yet, all the while, they're the one who acts in charge of things. Sagittarians need someone who is loving, sweet, and tender, who will let them do what they feel like doing and isn't nitpicky.

Sagittarians comes off as natural, quiet leaders and tend to fall in love with partners who are sweet yet strong. They hate silent, passive-aggressive tactics; if they do something stupid, approach them in that moment and just tell them what they've done wrong. They don't go for the shy, sensitive type. They need to feel that their partner can do fine without them. Only then will they stay.

❤ CAPRICORN IN LOVE

At times, Capricorns prefer a partner who is serious, while at other times they may prefer a lighthearted partner who will simply make them laugh. The latter will have an innocent quality—a purity—that Capricorn is drawn to. Which person Capricorn ends up with, though, depends on where they are emotionally and mentally. This is true for everyone to some extent, but it's especially true for Capricorn.

No matter how hard you make Capricorns laugh about themselves and the world, their path always leads back to the same riddle. Regardless of how hard they work, how far they climb, or how emotionally or physically rich they become, it's never enough. It only leads back to solitude or self.

Capricorns can be very independent. They don't like being told what to do or how to do it. They seem malleable and can get along with anybody, though they don't necessarily enjoy the company of just anyone. A partner must be stimulating; engaging; knowledgeable; and, most important, grounded in order for Capricorn to truly respect them. If Capricorns sense that their partner is off-kilter, they'll run for the hills. They won't try to change them or help as, say, Cancer would.

Tips

If Capricorn whispers evocative words about passion, love, and forever after, pay attention. They don't toss around romantic words just to attract you and then leave you cold. They have to be convinced in order to get involved. They're a little better at having meaningless flings than Virgos are, but eventually they'll want something that means family and future to them. And they take those ideas very seriously.

Capricorns respect those who are well informed. If you talk a good game and don't know your stuff, for example, forget Capricorn. They'll figure you out in no time!

Matches with Capricorn

Virgo may be too literal and spirited for Capricorn. Plus, Virgo in bed can bring out Capricorn's traditional side, which bothers Capricorn, who secretly longs for someone who can open them up emotionally and spiritually (both in bed and out).

Taurus may be too fixed, but because they both have the earth element in common, Capricorn and Taurus can get along well.

Of all the water signs, the intensity of Scorpios may be overwhelming—though Capricorn will get a real kick out of Scorpio's tendency to be jealous. In bed, these two can be smoldering.

The ambivalence of Pisces will, most likely, drive Capricorn nuts.

Capricorns may get along with Cancer because they're both cardinal signs, but these two can be competitive. Cancer and Capricorn both have refined senses of humor. A Capricorn must have patience to deal with Cancer's moods (which isn't likely).

Strangely enough, a Leo might be the best bet for Capricorn. If Leo has some earth in their chart—or some balanced air—they get along well. Certainly, the attraction is there. Capricorn mystifies Leo. Capricorn praises Leo the way they need to be praised.

— ✦ *Magical Musings* ✦ —

During Capricorn season, much of the world celebrates the end of the year and the start of a new year. Many witches, however, view Samhain, or Halloween, as the beginning of their yearly practices.

♥ AQUARIUS IN LOVE

Aquarians need the same space and freedom in a relationship that they crave in every other area of their lives. Even when they commit, this need doesn't evaporate. They must follow the dictates of their individuality above all else. This stubbornness can work against them if they aren't careful. Aquarians usually are attracted to people who are unusual or eccentric in some way. Their most intimate relationships are marked by uniqueness.

Aquarians can be very instinctive, but this doesn't mean they're self-aware. They also try to root for the underdog, but sometimes they pick the wrong underdog or victim to defend. Their upbeat, positive outlook on life can be tempered by idealistic notions they try hard to suppress. Their biggest goal in life is to remain calm and cool. This is very important for Aquarius because, when they let loose, they can be a fireball. If they get too wound up, the aggression they exude can be harsh for other people to cope with. Instinctively, they know this and try to temper it, often unsuccessfully.

Aquarians know they're strong individuals and that they can turn the tides in their favor. Luck follows them everywhere— even if they're not aware of it. They may even sense where they're headed before the fact. An Aquarius is not a big mystery, though. If you want an answer about love, just ask. Aquarians will tell you if your relationship is headed somewhere or not. If they're not sure, chances are that the answer is no, but they can be swayed over time.

Aquarians are survivors. So, if you want to be with one, know that they're hardheaded with their decisions. Under that cool exterior is a person who must, eventually, follow their heart and mind. This can be difficult, too, because the two forces don't always agree! But sticking with an Aquarius will pay off. They'll trust you and slowly get attached.

Aquarius also must see a bit of the world before settling down. They may even get married a couple times before realizing that they weren't ready for what they thought they were. An ideal partner for Aquarius will show their own mental agility, their independence, and their emotional strength of will. These traits will get an Aquarius to follow you to the ends of the Earth, but only if they're ready for something real to enter their life.

Tips

Aquarius loves to shock! They test people to see how smart and cool they'll be when they realize they've been teased. If someone overreacts or is too sensitive to this test, Aquarius will lose interest. It's all part of being fascinating, interesting, and fun for Aquarius. They have to know you'll play the mental games they love to play—and that you're strong enough to handle them. Therefore, don't get angry when Aquarius tests you. Laugh about it—and do it back. Aquarius will appreciate this!

Aquarius is impressed with bold, aggressive moves. Just make sure you have the mental connection first, or you'll be wasting your time. Aquarians are capable of having sex or a fling without getting emotionally connected at all. They won't judge you if you sleep with them right away, usually, but if you get overly romantic or clingy when Aquarius isn't quite as into it as you are, they will definitely back away from the situation.

Like Aries, Aquarius always needs a challenge on some level in all their relationships—or they won't take you seriously. Remember, Aquarius is a survivor and knows that nothing worth having comes too easily.

If Aquarius is not getting what they want out of the relationship, they're more likely to cheat than any other sign. Aquarius, like Sagittarius, will only be faithful to The One—and, even then, it may be difficult for an Aquarius to be completely and utterly devoted.

If an Aquarius has a short fling, or encounter, it doesn't mean their heart will be in it. Aquarians can turn their emotions on and off, but only when they're not in love. When they're in love, it's another story altogether.

Matches with Aquarius

Aquarians aren't prejudicial, so they usually get along with just about everyone. They're particularly attracted to people with whom they share intellectual camaraderie, people who make them laugh and make them feel good about themselves. In this way, Gemini can be a fabulous match for Aquarius, as long as they don't butt heads. This relationship can work only if the two find balance between neediness and independence. Also, Gemini can be extremely jealous and possessive with mates, which Aquarius abhors.

Aries is usually a good match for Aquarius. Together, they have lively, fascinating conversations, plenty of spirit, and mental camaraderie. Unfortunately, Aquarius will usually recognize Aries' flakiness factor, and then they're not sure if they can trust them. However, they like the challenge.

Many Aquarians wind up with Virgos. Virgos have the kind of stubbornness and organized stability that Aquarians secretly crave. But this may also be an ego thing. Remember, Aquarius loves a challenge, and Virgo keeps them squirming with their moral lectures and hardheaded ways. But, mentally and in bed, these two can do very well together.

A Libra or another Aquarius can be a good match, especially if one is more outgoing and gregarious than the other and lets their partner shine. Aquarians are usually secure enough to see bad and good traits in a partner that are similar to their own and still be able to deal with them and move ahead with the relationship.

A sign that's sextile or trine to Aquarius will also work. And Aquarius's polar opposite, Leo, can be an interesting mate for

Aquarius. If Aquarius doesn't get too self-involved and gives Leo enough attention, this can work. But Leo is usually running after Aquarius, and Aquarius can get bored of that—fast. If Leo pulls away a little, this pair can function well.

All in all, Aquarius is a great partner if you've truly won their heart. If not, you'll just be a stop along the way for lively Aquarius, who craves adventure and experience.

✦ *Magical Musings* ✦

It is not surprising to find a witch with a few planets in the sign of Aquarius. Aquarius is common among people interested in counterculture because they tend to follow their own path instead of dominant societal trends.

♥ PISCES IN LOVE

For some Pisceans, romance can be the point of transcendence— the stage in which they penetrate to the larger mysteries that have concerned them most of their life. To be romantically involved with a Pisces is to be introduced to many levels of consciousness and awareness.

There is nothing weak about Pisces, as many astrologers claim. Instead, Pisces watches from a distance and determines the best point of attack. Pisces may seem sweet and kind, but know this: When Pisces is in a relationship, and feels comfortable, there is no one who can manipulate you and your feelings like Pisces can (except, maybe, Cancer). Pisces knows how to play cold and walk away until you follow. A Pisces knows that this tactic usually works in human nature and has this move down to a science.

Pisceans are ten times craftier than they appear. They're incredibly good at hiding this side of themselves, and they're so adept at playing along with you, and seeming like they're on your side, that you won't even know what hit you when they use something you've told them against you in the future.

Pisces will test you. All Pisceans know how to challenge and how to get the answer they're looking for at the moment. If you're smart enough, you'll recognize this and pass the test. If not, Pisces will turn away without warning and find someone worthier of their affections.

Pisceans are idealistic…but they are dreamers with a vision. Most know what they want and go after it with a kind of slow, methodical gait. Eventually, most of them get what they want, even if it takes time. But they instinctively know how best to get the most out of their astonishingly calm composure and patience.

Pisces includes a little bit of every sign and can usually pull talents out of this grab bag at will. They can be a little mysterious like Scorpio, play noble like Leo, stand up with a commanding attitude like Sagittarius, be the charmer like Gemini, and act the part of smooth talker like Aries. The only role that Pisces has difficulty playing is Aquarius, whose sign sits next to Pisces.

In fact, Pisceans have a hard time hiding disdain for those they don't like. Pisceans have a regal air about them like Leo. But while Leo is more caring and noble, Pisces has a proud, capable, and studious air, which, try as they may, they cannot shake.

Pisces is intelligent and sympathetic. Don't ever confuse empathetic with sympathetic, though. Pisces will not feel your particular brand of sadness, though they seem to. Instead, they're likely to bring you out of the despair by understanding your plight and giving you good advice for it. But the sadness they show you will never reach their heart.

Tips

Pisces also has a thing for power. If you're someone they can look up to and admire, you'll win Pisces's heart. Unlike the air signs—Libra, Gemini, and Aquarius—Pisces will be more won over with accomplishment and quiet romantic gestures than by pure physical beauty.

Since Pisces likes the cool and understated, your manners, gestures, and even dress should be tasteful and elegant, not showy or ostentatious. The way someone puts themselves together will be more important to Pisces than makeup or any other superficial traits. Pisceans also appreciate directness and energy. They love intensity and romance, in a grounded and refined way.

Matches with Pisces

Other water signs seem the obvious choice here. But Scorpio might overpower Pisces, and Cancer might be too clingy. The signs sextile to Pisces are Capricorn and Taurus. While Capricorn might be too limited and grounded for the Piscean imagination, Taurus probably fits right in. Gemini, because it's a mutable sign like Pisces, also can be compatible.

Sagittarius may be the best combination for Pisces. Though appearing opposites, they complement each other quite well.

Pisces is able to soothe the Sagittarius savage beast; they let Sagittarius do what they want, yet they always keep the upper hand with a cool, polished, quietly strong demeanor. This is what Sagittarius likes best. As for the other fire signs, there doesn't seem to be much chance for them, but it really depends on the other factors in the two separate charts.

≋ SPELLBINDING SEX ≋

If your romantic relationship has moved beyond flirty friendship to a deeper commitment that could include intimacy, you might be wondering if the two of you are as compatible as lovers as you are as friends. What if you desire a slow, sensuous, and tender sexual encounter but your partner prefers a lightning-hot, muscular romp? Or, while you think that a dreamy sexual fantasy is almost as satisfying as the physical experience, they counter that hot and frequent sex is a healthy tension release. Knowing how each astrological sign approaches intimacy and expresses passion in relation to your own sign can enhance your understanding and intensify the experience when the moment is right.

ARIES

Sex with impatient, adventurous Aries can be dramatic and happen fast, so don't expect long-lasting foreplay. Aries are aroused by seeing the clothes come off. They love to be pleasured and can even be selfish lovers. Ever the bold trailblazers, they will try anything new at least once. With this sign, expect fireworks. If you want a faithful Aries, try to stay away from those who have their Venus (their love sign) in Aries, Sagittarius, or even Aquarius. They tend to wander. If you're an earth sign, pick an Aries with lots of air in their chart—they'll be drawn to you. If you're a water sign, you'll probably do well with Aries if they have a lot of fire.

TAURUS

If you're into languid, sensual lovemaking, a Taurus is for you. However, if you bed a Taurus too quickly, you'll lose their respect. The sensual Taurus wants to make love—a slow, seductive tango—that culminates in sex. Even if Taurus likes to talk dirty, they still want to know that the feelings there are real before they'll loosen up and be themselves in bed.

Taurus is compatible with Virgo and Capricorn and with water signs. Taureans are fatally attracted to Scorpios, their polar opposites. Although their elements, earth and water, should make them compatible, this tends to be a superficial connection. Instead, beneath the surface, they are at war with one other. But this kicks up the chemistry on a physical level.

— ✦ *Magical Musings* ✦ —

For spells that you want to last, cast them during a Taurus Moon, when the energy is consistent and calm. This patient energy may not burst onto the scene, but once it begins to take hold, it will stay the course.

GEMINI

Gemini is the biggest flirt in the zodiac and plays sexy to the hilt. They'll flirt in front of you and exude charm like you've never seen (except perhaps from a Libra). They'll be faithful after you've won their heart, though. Unfortunately, this isn't an easy task. Gemini will always go for the coolest person in the room, unless they're serious about settling down. Then they'll choose the person who grounds them. Engage them in an intriguing or interesting conversation—then leave and make it appear you are having a wonderful time without them. This may be a game, but it works. When Gemini finally realizes you've bailed on them, they'll come looking for you.

CANCER

In bed, the Cancer lover becomes a nurturer—gentle, thoughtful, and protective. They won't tell you what turns them on during sex; you are expected to intuitively know. They'll try new positions if they think it will please you. The erogenous zones of this sign are the stomach and breasts. When Cancers give their heart, expect them to be sweet, attentive lovers. Even if you are the initiator and a little aggressive in bed, don't worry, as they'll like it.

LEO

An erotic call at three o'clock in the morning, a chopper ride over Manhattan, five dozen roses that arrive at your office— these might be Leo's prelude to lovemaking. They like to do things in a royal manner that makes a dramatic statement and gets your attention. They are sensual creatures who like luxury and believe you get what you pay for. This lover understands the difference between paying for a $300 hotel and a $500 hotel; if you'd prefer to stay in a mud hut with no air conditioning or heat, you'd better find another Sun sign to share your bed. If you want to turn them on, make them think that you see them as a god or goddess. Leos enjoy their sexual trysts and pleasure their lovers well because they want to be seen as the best in bed.

VIRGO

Virgos, like Taureans, need to feel some kind of purity and sweetness in order to make love. They'd rather be in love than not and sometimes won't even have sex unless they're feeling love. You have to make Virgo feel special, or sex just won't happen. They can have adventurous affairs. However, as they get to know themselves, they'll simply want more from you and will despise the thought of getting close if you don't love them as much as they love you. This is a sign that sees sex as a release from daily tension, a healthy outlet that is necessary for one's well-being. In bed, this sign is sweet and considerate and can get turned on just knowing how much you appreciate them.

LIBRA

Although Libra can be aroused by a little role-playing or sex games, don't try it until the relationship is on equal footing. Libra seeks balance always, and this goes for bedroom activities. They'll eagerly give, and you'll receive, but it has to work both ways. Libra is often idealistic and overly sensitive. Additionally, it takes a Libra awhile to reveal themselves to you. You may find it difficult to deal with their constant back-and-forth of letting themselves go and reining themselves in. But ultimately, Libras are charming and make wonderful lovers when you make them happy and meet their needs.

SCORPIO

Suggest smearing their body in chocolate syrup from the neck down, and Scorpio might just go for it. Their intensity is legendary, and that extends to the bedroom. They like very sexy, yet tasteful, options. Scorpio can be the pleasure-seeking lover with strong fantasies. They will try new and different things involving intimacy. They'll keep your secrets and expect you to keep theirs. Scorpios will have flings with ultrasexy individuals, but they will never marry them.

Forget chasing after them. Scorpio needs to woo their partner. They may do it subtly at first, but eventually they'll invite you for a weekend away somewhere special. If they want you for their mate, Scorpio will be relentless in their pursuit until they get what they want.

SAGITTARIUS

Sagittarius is adept at separating sex and love. They are a passionate fire sign; however, sleeping with you doesn't necessarily equate with being in love with you. Ask them directly (not in a needy way); they will tell you frankly and won't mince words. They're good athletes, and that fitness extends to the bedroom. Get them turned on with a pillow fight or a tickling match. This is an ardent lover, more sensitive than they appear. Although they will care for any individual with whom they get involved, they won't have patience for those who play hard to get. If you lie to them or express neediness, it will only drive them out the door in search of a new lover. The way to keep them is to make them guess. Use direct words or quiet emotions. Sagittarius likes a subtle steering toward love.

CAPRICORN

To arouse a Capricorn, use a three-pronged approach—combine sexiness with conservativeness, and dress for the occasion. Capricorns appreciate a lover with confidence and know-how. They are often attracted to mature lovers, older than themselves. Such a relationship provides a sense of stability and security that Capricorns prefer over mercurial fireworks. Sex for them is straightforward, in keeping with the earthiness of their sign. Above all, Capricorn wants a loyal, stable, solid, and devoted partner. This lover needs to know that you'll be there when they need you, or they'll never consider you for the long term. Once in a relationship, Capricorns have a tough time walking away.

AQUARIUS

Getting an Aquarius hot and bothered might work better from a distance, through sexting or phone sex. Lovers of this sign possess a detachment that can drive you crazy at times. However, if you show the same detachment toward your Aquarian, it might actually serve as an aphrodisiac. For some Aquarians, the whole idea of sex and sexual fantasy appeals more than the actual act.

PISCES

Pisces is a sensitive and expressive lover with a seemingly supernatural depth of perception. They will do anything for their mate. Piscean sexual fantasies are richly imagined. They prefer show to tell when it comes to lovemaking. If love is absent, the Piscean can view the relationship with astonishing coldness, even if they find it difficult to break away. Still, they will love you forever, or at least tell you that. Pisces, like Cancer, has a tough time deciding what they truly want. There's something always in the back of a Pisces's mind that says "I could probably do better." And, because of their idealism, they'll always wonder what kind of partner they'd have in a perfect world.

A MATCH MADE IN THE STARS

Astrology as a field of study is illuminating and comprehensive but also expansive, meaning that there will always be more to learn. Nonetheless, you are now in a position to apply everything you've learned about astrology to your love life. Think about the tendencies of each sign as you meet potential partners, and use your intuition to see whether they'd be a good fit for you and your sign.

The love you've always wanted lies ahead. While your destiny may be written in the stars, the modern witch still has free will, so it is up to you to decide what kind of love you will claim and manifest.

— *Chapter 4* —

SPELLS:

ENCHANT YOUR WAY INTO YOUR PARTNER'S HEART

Spells are a tool that you can use to make your love life thrive, whether that means attracting a partner that is right for you or allowing for a deeper, more spiritual connection with someone you already know. When done with care and honest intention, spells can be instrumental in your quest for true love. Spells do not need to be complicated or include hard-to-find ingredients—sometimes the simplest spell is simply a spoken intention for love! This chapter will help you learn how to combine your intentions about love with the energy around you (which you can enhance with certain ingredients or incantations) to achieve the outcome you want.

THE ENERGY BEHIND SPELLS

At their core, spells are a combination of different energy frequencies used to attract what you want in life. Everything in the universe has an energetic frequency or signature note—each plays its own unique sound. These sounds can interact with those around them until everything is playing a beautiful symphony or an offbeat cacophony of sounds.

Spells work through the law of attraction, or like attracting like. The spell, with each of its energetic ingredients creating its own unique frequency, sends out a wavelength into the universe and seeks to find what is like it. Through this energetic shaping, you can bend and pull the fabric of the universe to help you find your magical match.

Each ingredient is added to a spell intentionally, specifically because of its distinct energetic signature. These frequencies work together to create a magical blend all their own. You may be asking yourself, how does this spell know to bring me the person of my dreams? The answer is, your intention!

INTENTION IS KEY

Before casting a spell, you need to set very clear intentions. You should think about the intention that you state outright and your internal—sometimes still unconscious—intention. This internal intention is going to do most of the work of directing your spell, that symphony of frequencies, out in the world—and for it to hit the right mark, the intention must be clear.

How do you set an internal intention based on feelings you might not even know about? You may need to do a quiet self-reflection before you start your spellwork. Do you perhaps have self-limiting beliefs that are getting in the way of your happiness? You may be surprised what you unearth. For example, the reason the individual in accounting, the one you have been hoping for weeks would ask you out, isn't giving you a second glance may be because you have an underlying fear of being with someone who could be smarter than you. Knowing that you have these underlying feelings will help you to craft a spell that is perfect for your unique situation. (In this case you might want to add a few ingredients to boost your self-confidence.)

You will also want to carefully consider the words used in your spell. The actual language should be crafted in a way that states your intention clearly and with purpose. Don't meander around the bush with your spell words—just say what you want.

— ✦ *Magical Musings* ✦ —

It is considered common practice to say the words "as the Universe sees fit" and "so mote it be" as a closure to your spells. This ensures the spell is being performed for the highest and best interest of those involved and nothing is done to work against anyone's free will.

Many spells use the elements of rhythm and rhyme to set the mood for casting, but this is not essential. Rhymes can help you remember a spell so that you can use it at a moment's notice, but, if you don't feel comfortable or can't think of a rhyme, don't worry. Remember, just focus on your intention of what you want, and the rest will fall into place.

CREATING A SACRED SPACE

A sacred space is a place for you to feel safe and comfortable, to escape from the pressures of the day, and to reconnect with your higher self. It can help you feel calm and centered. This is a place to go to when you want to do spiritual work—meditate, conduct palmistry, write in your journal, or cast your spells. Sacred spaces can be found or created anywhere, with any amount of space.

You can create your own sacred space by personalizing a particular room or portion of your home. A corner of a bedroom is a perfect place to use as a sanctuary. Add some decoration and color or surround yourself with treasures and trinkets that link with your heart. You can create a small personal altar or add a large sitting pillow so you'll be comfortable.

✦ *Magical Musings* ✦

When creating your sacred space, it is helpful to have a besom, or a ritual broom, handy to sweep out any unwanted energy that accumulates. You can use your besom before meditation or spell-work to prep the area for your magic.

If you are able to use the same space each time you cast a spell, the energy of the space becomes charged with your magical power and intention. The more you use your sacred space, the more the frequencies gather and collect. It then becomes your power zone, where you can gather more energy to send out into the world.

Activating Your Love Corner

In feng shui, your love corner represents space in your place that corresponds with your relationships. This space is located in every room, but it is important to pay particular attention to the love corner of your bedroom. To find your love corner, stand in the doorway or entrance to the room you wish to activate. Look straight ahead and then to your far right; this is your love corner.

Once you identify the corner, it's time to activate it. That means you'll consciously put items and decorations in this location that will promote relationships. There are many ways to activate your love corner:

✦ Place two chairs or two pillows to promote unions and healthy conversation.

✦ Place a crystal (such as a rose quartz or pink tourmaline) in that space to attract love.

✦ Light a candle in that area. Try a red or cinnamon-scented candle to ignite passion.

✦ Place an important picture in that area. (A picture of you and your partner is helpful if you want continued stability. Try to avoid pictures with only one individual for this location.)

✦ Consider adding small statues as activators. Those that symbolize union and love are especially nice.

When working with the love corner, take a moment to think about what type of love you are looking for and add items that speak to your specific desires. Be creative but don't clutter. Too much clutter will add to confusion and not allow the positive energy to flow. Less is more.

Once designed, activate your love corner. Activating the love corner stimulates the love sensors within yourself and your home to be more open and willing to receive all love. This corner also helps remove any obstacles that may keep you from receiving love.

To activate your space, try one of these options:

✦ Face your corner. Visualize yourself content in love. Think about your goal or vision. For example, if you desire a well-balanced marriage, then visualize yourself and your mate content, balanced, and living together in harmony.

✦ Hold and charge your crystal, visualizing your life complete in love.

✦ Hold and charge your candle. Once you see the full vision in your mind, light your candle. To keep your heart's desire afloat, continue to burn candles and light incense in that area to activate and draw love to you.

✦ Diffuse rose or geranium essential oil for general love.

CLEANSING YOUR TOOLS AND MATERIALS

Before you start performing spells in your new space, you will want to cleanse and charge any tool or ingredient you wish to use in a spell so that the vibrations are pure and ready for you to activate. You don't want the leftover energy of the clerk that sold you that pretty rose quartz muddying up your vibrational frequency stew you are concocting for your spell. There are many methods of cleansing and charging materials, but your intention to cleanse them is key.

✦ **To cleanse:** Using the light of the Moon is an easy way to cleanse or charge your tools. Remember to look up what phase the Moon is in so that you get the proper energy. A waning Moon, when the Moon is growing smaller in the sky, works well for cleansing magical tools. This releases the energy built up in the object.

✦ *Magical Musings* ✦ ---

Bells and singing bowls are also an easy way to cleanse any magical tool, especially when you do not have the right Moon phase available. Find a bell or bowl that emits a frequency that makes you smile and feels like it is releasing any gunk from around you. Trust your intuition and gut; you can't pick the wrong tone.

✦ **To charge:** To charge a magical instrument, place it under the light of a Full Moon. The Full Moon infuses the item with greater energetic frequency and power.

CLEANSING CRYSTALS

It is also important to cleanse any crystal before you use it. Many crystals are energetic sponges and can easily absorb the frequencies around them. You want your crystals clear and ready to do your bidding. There are a variety of methods that work well to cleanse a crystal. You can soak it in a mixture of salt and water or run it under the smoke of your favorite incense.

Some individuals even like to bury their crystals in the ground to cleanse them, but, if you go this route, make sure you remember where you put them!

—✦ *Magical Musings* ✦—

If you are going to dunk your crystal in water, make sure that it is not water-soluble first. A basic rule of thumb is if the crystal name ends in *ite* it will likely dissolve in water. Make sure to double-check with a quick search online or in your favorite crystal book. You don't want that new piece of selenite a few inches thinner after a bath in your favorite saltwater blend!

Grounding, Centering, and Shielding

It is essential to perform grounding, centering, and shielding prior to every type of spell or energy work. Your state of mind is elemental to the success of all spells. Grounding and centering gives the clarity and confidence necessary to complete any spellwork.

+ **Grounding and centering** focus your energy and direct it properly to what you want. If you are scattered, you won't be able to direct this energy to where it needs to go.

+ **Shielding** ensures that only positive energies aid you and keeps negative energies from invading your energy field.

Grounding

Grounding is the act of connecting your energy to Earth's through visualization and meditation. Think of grounding like a plant. Grow roots and become stabilized by the nutrients of Earth's energy. This process allows the energy in your body to balance and stabilize. By exchanging your energy with Earth's energy, you can cleanse yourself of negativity and excess energies. An overabundance of energy not channeled properly can cause problems. Grounding keeps you balanced with a continuous exchange. You can ground any time you feel spacey or disconnected. As you ground yourself, recognize what it feels like to be connected to Earth's energies. Some people feel a light swaying, while others feel a noticeable pull on the feet or spine. When you feel stable and connected, you are grounded. Here's a step-by-step exercise to walk you through the process:

GROUNDING EXERCISE

1. Find a place where you can sit quietly and comfortably with your back straight. Imagine yourself as a tree.

2. See yourself, glorious in wisdom and stability, beautiful with branches and leaves. Become aware of your legs and how they feel. Focus on your feet. See your feet grow roots. Let your roots grow and search thirstily through the Earth for its center. Reach down through the dirt and rock, down through the water table. See your roots reach the center of the Earth.

3. There, in the center, the spirit of the Earth is alive and pulsing with all her power and spirit. See this now. See her glowing in radiance and love, welcoming you to join with her. See this glowing orb of crystalline purity.

4. Allow your roots to reach around and grab hold of the crystalline orb. Secure yourself and become stable. Feel your roots adhere to the orb. Draw upon its energy. Bring it up through the tips of your roots. Drink in the energy from your roots up through the levels of the Earth. Feel the energy surge back into your body and all your appendages. Let yourself become purified and stabilized, free from all the negativity that clogs your heart. Feel rooted and grounded now. You are stable and secure.

Centering

Centering is the act of finding that quiet place in your heart and mind. It is being able to calm yourself despite your surroundings and daily misgivings. It is a focusing of heart, soul, and mind. Centering will allow you to empty your heart, soul, and mind of excess burdens. Try this exercise to center yourself.

CENTERING EXERCISE

1. Find a place where you can sit quietly and comfortably with your back straight. Relax. Focus on clearing your mind. It is natural for stray thoughts to pop into your head, but with practice you will learn to recognize and dismiss these errant messages without judgment. Centering will become easier each time you do it.

2. Visualize the color black first, to black out the noise and confusion. Once you feel the quiet, fade the black out.

3. Focus on the beating of your heart. See the whole heavenly universe. Know that it extends beyond all time and space. Visualize yourself existing in this space. Hear your heart beat, calm and steady. Enjoy the silence and sanctity of this infinite space.

4. Visualize an infinity symbol over your body, from head to toe. Imagine yourself tracing it, starting at the top of your head and following it to the bottom of your feet. Allow it to surround you and bring together your mind, heart, and soul.

5. Say to yourself: "I am balanced, I am centered." Begin to fade back to consciousness while retaining that clear and quiet mind.

SHIELDING

Shielding is the act of giving your personal space protection from negative energies that drain and feed off your energy field. This negativity is called psychic attack or psychic debris. Psychic attack and debris deplete your energy field, resulting in headaches, fatigue, and other ailments.

Feel free to use shielding throughout your daily life. Shielding also helps in the upkeep of the first two exercises, as a way for the energy you have just balanced and gained to sustain itself for longer periods of time.

There are many good visuals for shielding when you want to charge your aura with protection. You can visualize a suit of armor, a crystalline egg, or a bubble of light. Intention is everything, and it must stem from love. Whatever method you use to shield yourself, keep your mind focused and clear to properly shield. Follow these steps:

SHIELDING EXERCISE

1. Start the shielding exercise by breathing in through your nose and out through your mouth.

2. Recite the following prayer to ask for archangel Michael's help and protection:

> "Archangel Michael,
> I call upon thee,
> Send down a pillar of light to me,
> Protect me here and now from psychic attack,

Shield me from negativity,
And protect and watch over me.
I ask this for my highest and best,
So mote it be."

3. Visualize beaming blue energy streaming down from the heavens, surrounding you in a beautiful ball of light. Feel protected and shielded from any negative force. Feel only love in your heart and love around you.

4. Use this visualization technique anytime you feel the need for protection from negativity or psychic attack.

Once you feel comfortable enough with shielding, feel free to play and experiment with different visuals and affirmations to see what works best for you.

Appropriate Days and Lunar Times for Love Spellwork

Timing is everything. Choosing the right time of day and month can drastically affect success in spellwork. Each day of the week and part of the lunar cycle is associated with specific traits. Certain days are better for certain types of spells. Performing your spellwork on these days can enhance your success.

- **Sunday:** Ruled by the Sun, volunteer services, crops, and exercise.

- **Monday:** Ruled by the Moon, psychic development, feminine energies, family, health, and success.

- **Tuesday:** Ruled by Mars, business, animals, sex, passion, lust, and confrontations.

- **Wednesday:** Ruled by Mercury, communication, correspondence, and writers.

- **Thursday:** Ruled by Jupiter, self-improvement, prosperity, and social events.

- **Friday:** Ruled by Venus, love, passion, and creativity.

- **Saturday:** Ruled by Saturn, publicity, family ties, and self-improvement.

Another way to strengthen your spells is to perform magic during the proper Moon phases. Just as the days of the week affect spellwork, so, too, does the Moon. For magic, the lunar cycle is broken down into five main phases:

- **Full Moon:** Mother goddess energy, general magic, empowerment, prosperity, fertility, enhancement, bringing something toward you, issues that would need to work in your favor.

- **Waning Moon:** Crone goddess energy, removal of obstacles, release work, and cleansing rituals.

+ **Waxing Moon:** Maiden goddess energy, new beginnings, brings something toward you, prosperity, love magic, sex magic, and communication.

+ **New Moon:** New beginnings. This is when there is no Moon in the night sky. This phase occurs exactly opposite the Full Moon. It is recommended to *not* perform magic on this day. Perform magic one day after.

+ **Dark Moon:** Banishing, deep meditation, breaking spells, and breaking negative habits. This occurs close to the phase of the New Moon, three days before the actual change of the phase.

How Color Affects Love Spells

Colors are a fun way for you to affect spells and add another vibrational frequency to your symphony to attract love. Certain colors are more appropriate for love, but just like in any relationship, many different attributes can help make it fulfilling. Get creative! With spellwork, you are only limited by your imagination. Think about color when you choose your clothes and select materials and ingredients for certain spellcrafts.

The following is a list of colors and their associations. Some colors have similar attributes and can act as substitutions under the right conditions.

- **Red:** The direction south, element of fire, passion, creativity, sexuality, courage, willpower, female fertility and flow of life, deep desire, severe healing.

- **Orange:** Attraction, charm, harvest celebrations, success of goals, the deity Oghma, concentration.

- **Copper/Bronze:** Career growth, business fertility, money.

- **Gold:** Sun deities and solar energies, masculine energies, financial riches, luxury, happiness; substitute for yellow.

- **Yellow:** The direction east, element of air, trade, travel, intellect, communications, joy, happiness.

- **Green:** The direction north, element of earth, nature, fertility, growth, rejuvenation, abundance, prosperity, stability, herbal magic, plants; helps to counteract greed and jealousy.

- **Blue:** The direction west, element of water, sea deities, truth, wisdom, tranquility, deep emotion, spirituality, healing, feminine energies.

- **Indigo/Violet:** The element of spirit, divination, prophecy, angels, psychic abilities, meditation, astral projection.

- **Magenta:** Life purpose or life path, magnetism.

- **Pink:** Love gods and goddesses, softness, romance, friendship, femininity.

- **Brown:** The element of earth, hearth and home, animal magic, grounding, conservation; substitute for green.

- **Black:** Deities of the underworld, banishment of evil and negativity, release of past traumas or breaking bad habits and addictions, protection.

- **White:** Purity, angels, the element of spirit, healing, heightened awareness and vibration, truth; substitute for any color.

- **Silver:** Moon magic, goddess color, female energies, spiritual and psychic workings; can be replaced by white or gray.

- **Gray:** Neutralization; stalemate color.

✦ Magical Musings ✦

Color is a fun way to infuse different vibrational energies and perform subtle magic no matter where you are. Look carefully at the colors you wear or have on you when you are looking to ask out that potential partner or go on a hot date. If a certain color you want to use does not look good against your skin tone, you can always paint your nails that color or pick undergarments to match the color you want to invoke.

When it comes to love, remember the many different areas that make a relationship work in a balanced way. Colors for love are typically pink, red, and white, but be creative and explore other options for certain needs. For example, if you are having an argument with your partner and are not sure how to resolve it, give yourself time to think about the solution without the argument festering. In this situation, choose the color gray to work with. Gray is a stalemate color. It is used to postpone a situation or neutralize influences. This might buy you some time to come up with a solution. A powerful combination is gray, the neutralizer, and yellow, the architect of communication.

Spells to Connect with a Higher Power to Find Love

Many witches like to invoke the power of higher love, different deities (gods and goddesses), and other benevolent beings to help them perform magic. This is not essential but can boost the effectiveness of your spells.

Various cultures look toward certain gods and goddesses for help with anything and everything. People ask for help in finding soul mates and becoming pregnant, and many of us find comfort in knowing a higher power is out there, willing and able to help. Deities add potency and versatility to the spellwork you create, personalizing it to suit more of your own needs.

Finding a God or Goddess to Connect with

You may not feel worthy of accepting help from a divine source, but you are. By letting go of ego and allowing only feelings of unconditional love to enter your mind and body, you open yourself to receiving help and love from all benevolent beings. All you have to do is ask.

Finding your own god or goddess isn't as hard as you think. There are many resources available today regarding deities. Knowledge abounds. Search the Internet, scour your local library, or browse a New Age bookstore to find information. Expand your search to include cultures from all over the world. If you choose a deity from a culture you are not familiar with, be prepared to do some extra research to educate yourself about your deity's roots. It will be easier to establish a rapport with your deity and honor them properly if you know about his or her attributes and influences.

As you research, you will be able to decide which deity is right for you. Take a moment to think about what exactly you are looking for in the realm of love—marriage, passion, fertility, and so on. If you want to heal your marriage, you will choose a different deity from someone who is looking for a carefree sex life or someone who is searching for a soul mate. Choose a deity you feel comfortable with. The hard part is narrowing down the many options and selecting a specific god or goddess you connect with.

Another option is to make a connection with a benevolent being such as an angel or spirit guide. These good beings exist specifically to help others.

By creating a connection with a deity or being, you can magnify the intention you are trying to produce with extra power and potency. They are here to help you achieve your heart's desires.

—✦ *Magical Musings* ✦—

Spirit guides are like your own personal team of entities on the other side offering support and guidance. They were with you before you were born, and some will stay with you throughout this lifetime. If you don't feel comfortable connecting with deities, call on your own personal spirit guide to help.

Signs You Have Made Contact

Once you have chosen a deity or being, you need to find a way to communicate with them. (The spells later in this chapter are a great starting point!) Each deity prefers different means of communication, and you need to be alert to recognize your deity's messages. During the connection process, you may feel different sensations. These signs are usually slight changes in your senses, ranging from tingling feelings to new smells. However, they may be spiritual or emotional rather than physical. Here are some common signs of contact:

+ **Sight:** Sparkles or flashes of colors may appear to you, or light, quick visions seen in your mind's eye. You may experience flashes of images or nice thoughts and memories. Look at these thoughts as messages. What are they showing you?

+ **Smell:** What do you smell? A deity's smell, usually of flowers or incense, is always soothing. The smell will come out of nowhere and disappear as quickly as it came. Incense, flowers, and scents can also be associated with people you know who have passed.

+ **Taste:** Is there a strong taste in your mouth? This is usually consistent with sense of smell, which is connected to taste.

+ **Touch:** Think about what you feel. Some people report feeling sensations across the upper back and shoulders, while others feel tingling all over. Do you feel pressure on your shoulders or head?

+ **Emotional:** Overwhelming feelings of love and peace are common. Some people are even moved to tears.

Try not to force feelings or images. You may experience something completely different than the norm. Erase all expectations, but be aware that your deity or being will try to contact you. When you have a feeling or sensation, acknowledge it. It is important to keep an open mind and be of pure heart when calling upon any deity or benevolent being. Let's talk about how to find a god or being that's a good fit for you and your needs.

Goddesses Associated with Love

The goddess is referred to as the female aspect of the All. She is coruler in the heavens with the god, and together they make up the All Existence, sometimes referred to as "the Source." The goddess embodies the female energies and aspects of the human form. She is known by many names, among them Mother Earth, cocreator, the womb, and triple goddess. Following are goddesses related to love, with a little background and history regarding each.

— ✦ *Aphrodite* ✦ —

Aphrodite is the Greek goddess of love, beauty, and passion. She is said to be the most beautiful of all goddesses, and those who see her are mesmerized by her. Her primary role is to bring love into the world. According to Greek mythology, Aphrodite was the daughter of Uranus, the god of the sky and the heavens. Uranus was castrated, his testicles thrown into the sea, and Aphrodite arose fully formed from the sea-foam. Aphrodite was married off to the god Hephaestus, but she did not confine herself to her husband to satisfy her lust. Frustrated, Hephaestus crafted an unbreakable net and surprised Aphrodite and her lover Ares in the act of love. He summoned the rest of the gods to come and mock the lovers, but it did not deter them. Aphrodite remained married to her husband, despite her frequent extramarital affairs.

Aphrodite is always eager to help lovers. She is more a goddess of lust than of true love, but she is capable of falling deeply in love, even if her marriage to Hephaestus was a loveless union. She is quite jealous of other women, goddesses and mortals alike, and she is fiercely protective of her offspring.

APHRODITE'S LOVE POTION

In this spell, you mimic a love potion created by Aphrodite to tip her son Eros's arrow for love magic. It will bring love to you when you wear it. You'll need:

* 1 sheet rice paper
* 1 pen with red ink
* 1 (1-ounce) cobalt glass bottle with cover
* 3 drops musk oil
* 6 drops vanilla oil
* 1 ounce almond oil

1. Recite the following incantation to invoke Aphrodite for help in your quest to find love.

"Beautiful Aphrodite, loving and kind,
Trigger in me only that which is divine.
Send to me love, pure and true.
Bless this oil, through and through."

2. Write on rice paper the qualities you desire in a mate.
3. Roll your message into a tight scroll, and place scroll into bottle.
4. Add combined drops of musk and vanilla oil into bottle. Fill remainder of bottle with almond oil.
5. Hold and charge. Visualize yourself fulfilled with your desired love.

6. Anoint yourself with the oil every day and recite the following incantation for as long as needed:

"Aphrodite, come to me.
Aphrodite, bring love to me,
For my highest and best interest.
So mote it be."

— ✦ Hera ✦ —

Hera is the Greek goddess of love and marriage, wife to Zeus, and coruler of the gods and heaven. Call upon Hera when working on protecting your marriage. She is wonderful at helping to find love and at maintaining a strong and healthy relationship. (She is also a great patron goddess to single women because of her strength and independent nature, however. Hera has always risen above challenges she's faced in relationships, proving that she can make it on her own.) Because she represents honesty and truth within a relationship, she will protect your heart—making her an excellent goddess to turn to for help during times of infidelity. She has had firsthand experience dealing with infidelity, as Zeus is known for his wandering eye. She can give insight and patience to those in a similar situation.

Hera is considered a mother goddess, and she is always depicted as beautiful with large eyes. She also brings fertility and protection for children.

HERA'S FIDELITY POUCH
*

This spell is designed to strengthen the bond between couples to promote fidelity. For best results, perform this spell on a Sunday. Gather these ingredients:

* 1 white cloth, 4"–5" diameter
* Dried white rose petals
* 2 tablespoons mint
* 1 teaspoon ground myrrh
* 1 piece amber
* White leather lacing
* 2 blue pony beads
* 1 peacock feather

1. Lay white cloth flat. Layer rose petals, mint, and myrrh on the center of the cloth.
2. Hold and charge amber stone by visualizing the bond between the individuals strengthened in love and fidelity. Place amber in the center of the herbs.
3. Close cloth to create a pouch and tie with lacing. Secure the ends by threading pony beads through lacings. For the final touch, thread the end of the peacock feather in between pony beads and leather lacings.
4. While holding your bundle, recite the following incantation as you think of you and your partner:

"Hail to goddess Hera of marriage and love,
Gaze at us from Mount Olympus above,
Empower this bundle and guide us in life,
Strengthen our bonds through times of strife.
Devotion, purity, and truth to be,
These for a healthy partnership, happy and free."

5. Hang the bundle on or above your bed, or place it by a nightstand, for as long as the relationship needs.

✦ *Magical Musings* ✦

If you have trouble finding any spell ingredient at your local stores, just look online. There are a lot of specialty websites that carry ingredients specifically for the modern witch.

GODS ASSOCIATED WITH LOVE

Gods are the male aspect of the higher love, often referred to as the cocreators. For centuries, society has looked toward the gods to bring about change within family life, from creation to protection. A god is a goddess's counterpart, differing only in his masculine aspects. Following are some gods who are worshipped or called upon to help bring about love.

— ✦ Eros ✦ —

Eros, the Greek god of love, is more commonly known by his Roman name, Cupid. As the son of Aphrodite, he helped his mother in the quest for love. It was Eros's job to shoot the unsuspecting victim with an arrow, which was tipped with a special love potion created by Aphrodite. The potion would make the victim fall immediately in love with the next person they encountered, giving birth to the timeless phenomenon of love at first sight.

CUPID'S ATTRACTION SPELL
— ✴ —

This spell is designed to attract an appropriate mate for you. It mimics the story of the potions Aphrodite made to tip Eros's arrows. For best results, perform on a Friday during a waxing to Full Moon.

* 1 unscented red votive candle
* 1 toothpick
* 1 cotton ball

* 1 drop clove oil
* 4 drops bergamot oil
* 2 drops lavender oil

1. Hold and charge candle by visualizing attracting your ideal mate. Think about all the attributes you would want in a mate to complete you and provide a balanced relationship. See your partner finding you easily and overcoming any obstacles. See that journey extend through time and space so your partner will be awakened to you, no matter where they are now.

2. Using toothpick, carve into candle a heart with a double-ended arrow shooting through the center.
3. Combine oils on cotton ball and anoint candle and symbol. For added potency, wear the oil as a perfume every day until your mate arrives.
4. Recite the following incantation while lighting candle:

"Cupid, Cupid, come to me,
Sling and set your arrow free,
Travel long and travel far,
Hit the mark right on the heart.
Attract and find my mate to be,
Quickly, steadily, come to me."

5. Burn candle down completely to ensure full potency. Should time be a concern, choose a smaller candle or snuff out candle to seal in its energies. Repeat the incantation each time you relight your candle.

— ✦ Aengus ✦ —

Aengus is a Celtic god of love, soul mates, marriage, and poetry. He is known by many as "the young god" and is often depicted with four birds flying over his head, symbolizing kisses.

One night, Aengus dreamed of a beautiful young maiden named Caer. He fell in love with her and vowed to find her. With his parents' help, Aengus managed to track down his true love. He arrived at a lake called the Dragon's Mouth to find 150 maidens chained together. The maidens transformed into swans on the first of November every year, and Aengus had to identify his beloved in her avian form in order to win her. Aengus transformed himself into a swan and recognized Caer. They flew off together and sang a sweet melody for three days and three nights.

DREAMING OF LOVE

This dream-pillow spell opens your third eye (your center of intuition located between your eyebrows and up an inch) to allow you to "see" your love, which will help you find and attract your soul mate. For best results, conduct this spell in November, beginning three days prior to the Full Moon and ending three days after the Full Moon. Sleep with your pillow every night.

* ¼ cup dried peppermint
* ¼ cup dried lavender
* ¼ cup dried patchouli
* ¼ cup dried mugwort
* ¼ cup dried mullein
* ¼ cup dried vervain
* 1 tablespoon ground dragon's blood resin
* 1 Herkimer diamond crystal
* 1 (6" × 12") piece 100% cotton indigo fabric
* Needle and white thread
* 1 white feather
* Natural cotton filling

1. In a medium glass bowl, place peppermint, lavender, patchouli, mugwort, mullein, vervain, and dragon's blood. Mix them with your hands. With your hands, charge herbs with their purpose. Recite the following incantation while you charge herbs:

> "Open, open my heart will be,
> Open, open my eye shall be,
> Open, open I look and see,
> Open, open my love to be."

2. Let your hands hover over herbs. Imagine love pouring out of your hands and into herbs. Visualize herbs being charged with the intent to magnify your third eye to see and find your true love. Place herbs aside.

3. Hold and charge Herkimer diamond by visualizing. Empower this stone, projecting psychic qualities to allow you and your partner to see each other in your dreams by opening the third eye.

4. Fold fabric in half and sew two sides. Turn the pillowcase inside out.

5. Stuff pillowcase with herbal mixture, Herkimer diamond, and white feather. Finish stuffing pillowcase with natural cotton and sew closed. Recite the following incantation as you fill your pillowcase:

> "Aengus of love,
> Help me take a peek,
> Reveal to me the love I seek."

6. Sometimes it is difficult to remember dreams. Try stating an affirmation like this one to ensure memory recall:

> "I call upon my higher loves and angels to help me tonight.
> Help me remember my dreams throughout the night."

7. Write your dreams in a journal to strengthen your memory recall.

Vervain is also known as devil's bane. This plant has a long history of being associated with the supernatural because of its protective qualities. Many spells use vervain as an ingredient against potential psychic attacks. It can also be added to spells to help restore a fading love.

SPELLS TO ATTRACT LOVE

The simple love spells in this section will help you attract the love you've been looking for. These spells are versatile and allow for substitutions so you can customize them to your specific needs. After looking at the spells, explore ways in which you can make them more personal, such as by choosing your favorite flower in place of the suggested bud or substituting an essential oil you are drawn to for an herb that you cannot find. This will empower your magical workings to their maximum effect.

You do not necessarily need to have a specific person in mind when you are casting these spells. The spell components use concentrated symbolization and associations to manifest the connection between two hearts.

SMALL-SCALE ATTRACTION GRID

*

This small crystal grid can be done anywhere it can be left alone, such as the sacred space you created. It only requires an area about the size of a dinner plate. Use small versions of the crystals listed, except for the activator crystal, which should be medium-sized in comparison to the surrounding crystals. This grid will help you attract a partner or help bring balance and active love in the home.

* 1 activator crystal (clear quartz will work, but choosing a crystal that is green or pink, such as green aventurine or rose quartz, would be ideal)
* 4 small clear quartz crystal points
* 1 picture (find a picture that represents the love you seek, such as a couple or two hearts together)
* Red pen
* 1 small rose quartz pyramid

1. Charge activator crystal by visualizing love entering into your life and filling your home while you hold it. Allow feelings of excitement to fill your heart.
2. Place one crystal point at each of the four points of a square, facing each other and in toward the center of your designated area, love corner, or altar.
3. Write your intention in red on the back of the photo. If you are looking to find love, write a description of your desired love on the back of the picture. Include physical attributes and hobbies. Be creative but realistic, and remember the laws governing free will. If you are seeking balanced love in a relationship, think about where balance needs to be and write it on the back of the picture. Hold and charge the photo.

4. Place picture in the middle of crystal grid, face up, and place rose quartz pyramid over picture. Visualize the pyramid sending a beam of rose-colored light into the universe. See your goal manifested.

5. Recharge crystals and photo each day. Perform this spell every month, starting on a Friday of a waxing to Full Moon, until you attract the love you seek.

✦ *Magical Musings* ✦

Pay attention to how you mix your spell ingredients. When you move something deasil, or clockwise, you allow energy to enter. When you mix your ingredients widdershins, or counterclockwise, you remove energy.

MESSAGE IN THE BOTTLE

This spell calls out to your long-lost love to come find you. It is best used to call for help from afar. You are summoning your love to come help complete your heart. The Lady of the Lake will bestow this message only upon the most worthy. Arthurian legend states the Lady of the Lake bestowed Excalibur upon the worthiest of men; think of your heart as Excalibur! You'll need to find a body of water for this spell—a local river, lake, or ocean would work.

* Piece of parchment paper
* Red pen
* 1 small bottle with cork
* Rose petals
* Assorted red, pink, and white beads
* Biodegradable glitter
* 1 water lily bloom

1. Write your love letter with parchment paper and red pen. This letter should contain your love needs, wants, and expectations. It should be written from your heart. Tell your soon-to-be lover you are waiting and have so much love to give and share. While writing, feel the energy you are charging with flow through you to your pen and onto the paper, where the ink will empower your desire.

2. Add the rest of the ingredients, except for the water lily bloom, to the bottle to add more potency for beauty, love, and romance.

3. Walk to the water's edge. While holding bottle over the water, recite the following incantation:

"Lady of the Lake, I summon thee,
Reach up and engulf me, take this message from me.
Empower and send this message of light
To only the worthiest of suitors, armor shining and bright."

4. Fill bottle with water. Visualize the Lady of the Lake rising up out of the water and transforming your message into energy. See the energy drain from the bottle into her hands, leaving only your ingredients. She will now take your message and present it only to the one worthy of your love.

5. Set your offering, a water lily bloom, atop the water to thank the Lady of the Lake.

VALENTINE LOVE LETTER SPELL

— * —

In this spell, pour out your emotions of love, romance, and passion to the one you desire. The letter and your words will help your heart connect with your lover's heart. Ask the god Oghma for help writing your letter. He is associated with the color orange for attraction, as well as all things poetic and lyrical.

This spell requires dove's blood ink, but don't worry; there is no actual blood in this ink. Dove's blood ink is a deep red pigment that is traditionally used in witchcraft, particularly in love spells. It is available widely online, but if you have trouble finding it you can substitute red ink.

* Parchment paper
* Dove's blood ink
* Quill or other fancy pen
* Fixative or adhesive spray
* Glitter
* Valentine confetti

* Favorite perfume
* 1 red envelope
* Red sealing wax
* Heart stamp
* 3 small orange-flavored cakes or preferred offering

1. Gather all your elements together. Ground, center, and feel the energy flow to charge your ingredients. Visualize these ingredients charged with bright white light. Empower this energy with the intent to draw in romance, love, and passion.

2. Recite the following incantation before you begin writing your love letter:

"Oghma, god of the bards,
Bless me with the right words to say what is in my heart,
And on my mind, and on my lips."

3. Compose your letter using the quill pen. Pour out your heart's desire. Speak truth and love, and fill your letter with prose and poetics. Visualize all of your love being absorbed with each letter, word, and phrase.
4. Decorate your letter. When you're finished writing, spray the fixative over the letter. Sprinkle and adhere glitter and magical Valentine confetti. Finalize your decoration with a topcoat of spray and let dry.
5. When dry, infuse with your essence by spritzing your favorite perfume on the letter.
6. Seal the letter in the envelope with the red sealing wax and stamp. Now it's time to decide what to do with it. If you have a specific person in mind, you can send it directly to them, from a secret admirer. If you would rather not send your letter to anyone, burn it under February's Full Moon, asking the universe to send your message of love along and release the magic into the universe.
7. Give thanks with orange-flavored cakes.

— ✦ *Magical Musings* ✦ —

Many witches in the northern hemisphere celebrate Imbolc in early February before Valentine's Day. Imbolc symbolizes the returning of the light after a period of darkness. This is a great time to cast spells to bring the light of a new romance into your life!

LOVE CANDLE SPELL

This spell is for a general welcoming of love into your life. Substitute with whatever color candle you want to use for a specific type of love. The pink candle in this spell represents love, friendship, and romance, but you could also use green to promote a healthy nurturing relationship or orange for a creative union in the bedroom. For best results, begin your spell on a Monday during the waxing to Full Moon.

* 1 pink unscented candle
* Toothpick

* Rose oil, or favorite essential oil blend

1. Hold candle and charge it by visualizing in your mind accepting and allowing love to enter your life in any and all forms while you hold it. Be open and receptive to all kinds of love that will come to enrich your life. See your heart become complete through the new love you will allow in.
2. Use toothpick to carve a heart in candle in one fluid motion. Connect both ends to create a complete heart, unbroken.
3. Anoint candle with oil, starting with the completed heart.
4. Recite the following incantation for the goddess to come to your aid in your request to allow new love into your life. (You may want to refer to the god and goddess information earlier in this chapter to expand upon or change the incantation to suit your needs.)

"Moon goddess, I call to thee.
Send down your light for guidance to me.
Let me be a part of your enveloping light,
Allowing my love to come into my life."

5. Light and burn candle completely. Should you not have enough time in one session, snuff out candle to keep the energies intact. Whenever you relight, simply restate the previous incantation and steps.

SYNERGY LOVE BLEND
— ✳ —

The following synergy love blend is created to attract love, romance, and friendship. The oils used for this particular synergy were selected for their association with love, as well as the smell they give off, which is appealing to many people. If you prefer, change up the oils to match your personal needs.

* Patchouli oil
* Sandalwood oil
* Lemon oil
* 1 ($^1\!/_2$-ounce) blue or amber-colored bottle, or cotton ball

1. Blend equal parts patchouli, sandalwood, and lemon to fill a bottle or dab onto a cotton ball.
2. Hold and charge the oil by visualizing it absorbing your love and desire. See yourself happy and filled with love.
3. Recite the following incantation while applying the oil:

"Love, love, come to me,
Love, love, so mote it be."

4. Apply as needed behind the ears and on the wrists and heart to activate and attract love to you.

Tarot Love Spell

This spell uses the symbolism in a traditional Rider Waite tarot deck. Focus on the energies in the suit of cups for love, happiness, and the life force of the emotional heart. For this spell, the cup image represents the holy grail as it relates to the bond of everlasting love and life. The king and queen of cups represent the female and male energies coming together to create a balanced and happy relationship—the image traditionally depicted on the ten of cups card. The path of energy, drawn and connected with the bloodstone, forms an upside-down triangle, echoing the shape of the chalice. Arrange and host this spell in a sacred space or altar, where it can work continuously without being disturbed.

* Queen of cups tarot card
* King of cups tarot card
* Bloodstone obelisk
* Ten of cups tarot card

1. Look at queen of cups and king of cups and choose the card that you feel most represents you, regardless of gender depicted on the card. Feel the energies and see which one you are drawn to. Hold and charge it with your energy. See and feel all the love from your heart filling this card and empowering it with the intent to send out love to connect with and attract a partner. Use the other card to represent your mate. Hold and charge. Empower this card with all the qualities you are looking for in a mate. See and feel all the love from your heart filling this card and empowering it with the intent to attract someone to you.

2. Place your cards in an upright position in a triangle form with your card and your mate's card forming the sides.

3. Hold and charge bloodstone. Empower its properties of manifestation and attraction. While holding bloodstone on top of ten of cups, visualize a beam of energy entering and surrounding the card, empowering the goal to manifest. Recite the following incantation:

"By the power of bloodstone, I empower thee!"

4. Move the stone, and hold it on top of the card representing yourself. Recite the following incantation:

"By the power of bloodstone, I empower thee!"

5. Move the stone, and hold it on top of the card representing your mate. Recite the following incantation:

"By the power of bloodstone, I empower thee!"

6. Move the stone, and hold it on top of the ten of cups once again. Recite the following incantation:

"And together we unite, three by three!"

7. See the completed energy path as a glowing triangle. Place the stone at the bottom of the triangle formation to represent the handle of the chalice.

8. Repeat this spell often to keep the energy in the chalice filled and flowing for the manifestation to work continuously.

THE SIREN'S CALL

The Siren's Call spell empowers your voice to be seductive and attractive to all those who hear it. The sirens, also known as sea nymphs, are often depicted as mermaids. Legend states that those who hear the song of the sirens are mesmerized by their beautiful voices. Call upon the sirens to bless and empower your voice so that it may resonate through the waters of emotion and love to find your mate. This spell requires visiting a shoreline of a pond, ocean, or stream.

* 1 seashell bead or seashell with a hole in it
* 16"–18" of black embroidery thread
* 1 embroidery needle
* Offering of your choice, such as honey, wine, or lavender

1. Walk to the water's edge. Hold seashell over the water, and recite the following incantation:

"Sing to me the songs of the sea,
That I may speak so lover'ly,
Send out this message of love for me,
Attract and find my love to be."

2. Scoop up water with your seashell to bless and empower it.
3. String the seashell onto the embroidery thread, and wear this charm to enchant your voice.
4. Leave your offering of choice at the water's edge, bidding farewell and gratitude to the sirens. When your necklace falls off on its own, your love has heard your call and is on the way.

Knot magic is an easy way to do magic in secret or on the go. You can use embroidery thread or any string you have near. As you say a spell, tie a knot in the string. This binds the magic. Untying the knot will release the energy back into the universe.

WINDOW TO YOUR SOUL
— ✳ —

This spell shines a light in your window for your soul mate to see, thus leading your soul mate home.

* 1 white pillar or seven-day candle
* 1 toothpick

1. Mark seven horizontal lines equal distance apart on candle with toothpick. Each line sections off how much to burn for each day so you can keep track for the seven-night stint.
2. Hold and charge the candle by visualizing the candle and flame becoming a beacon of light shining through time and space as you hold it. Visualize its brightness cutting through the darkness of the night for your soul mate to see.
3. Now visualize your soul mate. Feel the connection begin to grow between you both. Visualize a golden cord connecting the two of you. See your souls coming together at last, completing each other in mind, body, and soul.
4. Recite the following incantation each time you relight your candle.

> "Of seven days and seven nights,
> Twin souls created as one.
> We journey from afar to reunite.
> No longer separate, we are one."

5. Every night at seven o'clock relight candle and burn it down to the next line. Snuff out flame to seal in the magical energies.

PASSION INCENSE
——— ✳ ———

This incense stimulates sexual desire. Create and empower these ingredients under the energies of the Full Moon. By charging these ingredients with intent, you will magnify their qualities.

* ✳ 1 teaspoon cardamom seeds
* ✳ 1 teaspoon ground cinnamon
* ✳ 1/4 teaspoon ground cloves
* ✳ 1 tablespoon ground dragon's blood resin

* ✳ Mortar and pestle
* ✳ Hot charcoal briquette
* ✳ Ashtray or firesafe container

1. Grind ingredients with mortar and pestle. Visualize ingredients fusing to create a spicy, sultry combination.
2. See yourself aroused by the smell as it permeates the atmosphere. This aroma intensifies the feelings of passion surrounding you and your mate.
3. As you prepare the ingredients, recite the following incantation:

"Smoke and fire,
Swirling higher,
Wafting passion and desire,
As I inhale sweet smells above,
Divine will bless me with passionate love."

4. Burn incense when you want to invoke the power of passion. To do so, sprinkle powdered mixture over hot charcoal briquette in firesafe container. For added potency, recite incantation whenever you light incense.

LOVE DIVINATION
——— ✶ ———

This incense opens your third eye, allowing you to see and find your love-to-be. Be open to receiving any and all messages when performing the act of divination. This spell is best performed during a waxing to Full Moon on a Friday evening.

* ¹/₂ teaspoon dried lemon-grass
* ¹/₄ teaspoon dried sage
* ¹/₄ teaspoon dried mugwort
* 3 drops lavender oil
* ¹/₄ teaspoon dried patchouli
* 2 tablespoons ground dragon's blood resin
* 2 tablespoons ground benzoin
* Large mortar and pestle
* Charcoal briquette
* Firesafe container

1. Grind ingredients with mortar and pestle until they form a finely ground powder.

2. Empower ingredients by letting your hands hover above herbs. Visualize universal energy streaming from your hands and into herbs, charging them with intent.
3. Ground and center yourself.
4. Sprinkle mixture over hot charcoal briquette in firesafe container. Recite the following incantation:

> "Through smoke and air,
> The vision begins
> To show me where my love exists.
> Give me a symbol,
> Give me a sign,
> So I know where to look, love be mine."

5. Sit and meditate, breathing in through your nose and out through your mouth. Absorb the scent of the incense, and feel it expand your third eye. See and feel colors of light streaming in and out of your third eye, sending your message of love into the universe.
6. Relax and wait to see what the universe has to show you. Do not force anything.

— ✦ *Magical Musings* ✦ —

Mugwort is a common ingredient in many spells. This herb is known to increase psychic ability and is useful for divination. Try drinking a cup of steaming mugwort tea before practicing your psychic skills.

The Dance of Three

—— ✳ ——

The next spell is designed with simplicity in mind. The incantation, "the dance of three," will invite the winged faeries to carry your message of love on the wind. With longevity in mind, your words of love will find your lover's ear and attract that person to your life.

✳ 1 dandelion clock (a head that's ready to have its seeds blown)

1. Pick white dandelion.
2. Hold dandelion in your hand and focus the energy on attracting your life mate. Keep this thought simple and pure. Be open-minded, as you might not know who your life mate is.
3. While holding dandelion, recite the following incantation:

> "Dance with me the dance of three,
> The past, the present, and future to be.
> O dandelion and winged faerie,
> Send my love this message for me.
> That I am waiting so patiently
> For you to come and share with me,
> My love, my life, my future to be.
> For my highest and best interest
> What will be, will be."

4. Blow as hard as you can to release all the seeds into the wind.

Love Charms,
Talismans, and Sachets

Following are some creative ways of making your own charms, talismans, and sachets for attracting your mate. This style of spellcraft is fun to make, and they become everyday objects that you can wear or put in your bag or pocket. You can also leave them in your sacred space and charge them that way if you prefer. But by keeping them with you while you travel, the magic works wherever you go.

Lucky Love Bracelet

The ingredients for this simple binding spell are easily found in most craft stores. Feel free to sew on charms, beading, or even pretty stones or runes to accentuate your personal style. If you don't want to wear the bracelet, try fastening it to a keychain, tying it to a bag handle, or hanging it over your car's rearview mirror.

* 1 bundle white embroidery thread
* 1 bundle red embroidery thread
* 1 bundle pink embroidery thread

1. Cut three pieces embroidery thread, forearm length, for each color.
2. Braid white thread and set it aside. Do the same for red and pink threads. While you braid, recite the following incantation to seal in the intention to allow love into your life:

> "Love and light,
> Surround me in life."

3. Take your three separate braids and braid them into one. Again, recite the incantation as you braid.

— ✦ *Magical Musings* ✦ —

An athame is a witch's ritual knife. This tool can be used in spellcraft to cut items as well as to stir or mix ingredients together when you don't have a spoon handy. Ritual items have an energy to them that adds an extra vibrational ingredient to the mix.

UNDYING LOVE
— ✶ —

This spell opens your heart, allowing you to give and receive love. It calls the energies of the undines, the elemental beings of water, to impart the compassion and understanding of emotional love and help heal the heart, thus opening it to receive a deeper and more satisfying love. This spell works best if performed on a beach, but a large body of water such as a lake or stream will work as well.

* 1 beach rose
* Beach sand
* 1 small glass jewelry bottle pendant

1. Walk toward the water's edge and find a place to sit and experience the beach while you close your eyes and visualize.
2. Understand that your heart is like a rose, beautiful and deserving of admiration and love when opened to its true potential. See your heart opening like a rose coming to bloom.
3. When you feel your heart is opened to its full potential, release the flower into the water. Recite the following incantation:

> "Compassionate undines,
> Hear my plea,
> Open my heart
> To give and receive
> Pure love and light.
> So mote it be!"

4. While still at the water's edge, collect a small amount of beach sand in the little bottle.
5. Fill the remaining space with water.
6. Hold your newly made talisman out over the water before you go so the undines will bless it.
7. Wear the bottle around your neck so it will sit directly over your heart for as long as needed. Feel free to re-empower your spell whenever needed, remembering to cite the incantation for the undines' continual blessing.

ADAM AND EVE TALISMAN

Here we will mimic the fertility of Adam and Eve to aid you in your own fertility rites. Adam and Eve roots can be found in almost any herb shop and are called this name because of their similarity to the male and female sexual organs. Carry this root pair in a pouch wherever you go to attract and find happiness in love.

* 1 pair Adam and Eve roots   * 1 red pouch

1. Place the roots inside the pouch and tie it closed.
2. Empower each root to attract balance in happiness and love. When charging your talisman, recite the following affirmation:

> "Root from Eden, holy and divine,
> The gift of paradise will soon be mine.
> Like the apple or the fruit from the vine,
> Invoke the love that will soon be mine."

3. Wear or carry with you wherever you go. You just never know where love may happen!

Passionate Love Sachet

Empower your lingerie with this passionate energy sachet. For best results, perform this spell on the Friday of a waxing Moon.

* 1 (4" × 8") piece of white or pink lace
* Needle and pink thread
* ¼ cup dried rose petals
* ¼ cup dried lemon balm
* ¼ cup dried lavender
* 2 tablespoons cloves

1. Fold lace in half and sew two sides. Turn fabric inside out to create your sachet.
2. Combine herbs in a glass bowl. Charge and empower herbs with the intent that they activate passion within your life. See and feel love filling the herbs, charging them with this purpose.
3. As you fill your magical sachet, recite the following incantation:

"Romance and passion,
Ignite into my life.
Empower my drawers for a new love life.
Attract and bring passion to me,
A love life fulfilled in every way it will be."

4. Sew your sachet closed and place it in your lingerie drawer.
5. If you have leftover herbs, use them as an offering to the universe or sprinkle them on the threshold of your home to attract a mate to you.

ATTRACTION SACHET

This sachet is perfect for attracting love into your life and home. Perform this spell on the Friday of the waxing Moon. Call upon the god Quetzalcoatl, as he is the full embodiment of a god, and there is nothing in daily life that he can't help accomplish.

* 1 (4" × 8") piece of white lace
* Needle and white thread
* ¼ cup rose petals
* ¼ cup orange blossoms
* ¼ cup vanilla beans

1. Fold lace in half and sew two sides. Turn fabric inside out to create your sachet.
2. Combine ingredients in medium bowl.
3. Charge and empower herbs with the intent that they attract love and passion into your life. See and feel the universal energy come from your hands. Visualize the energy making your herbs glow with a glorious, attractive golden-orange light.
4. As you fill your magical sachet, recite the following incantation:

> "Quetzalcoatl! Hail to thee!
> Empower these herbs for love to be.
> Attraction, love, and soul search be done,
> Send me my mate; you are the god, you are the Sun."

5. Sew your sachet closed and place it near an entryway by hanging on the door handle or above the threshold.

≋ SPELLBINDING SEX SPELLS ≋

Sex spells are the most sensual and sultry form of intimate love magic. This is where partners become most vulnerable and share an act of love that is more than sex. The raw primal energies raised during lovemaking add immense power to magic. The spells and potions in this section are meant to manifest your sexual desires for your relationship. Combine any exercise, potion, and spell to drive your senses wild!

SENSUAL PILLOW SPRAY

—— ✳ ——

To spice up the bedroom, work with aromatherapy and the magical qualities of garnet to ignite passion in your life. This pillow spray is made with known aphrodisiacs, which are sure to entice the senses and invite raw sexual energy within your bedroom. Create this spell during a waxing to Full Moon.

* ✳ 1 small fine-mist spray bottle
* ✳ 10 ounces distilled water
* ✳ 2 ounces vodka or white vinegar
* ✳ 3 drops patchouli oil
* ✳ 6 drops vanilla oil
* ✳ 1 drop peppermint oil
* ✳ 1 small garnet

1. Fill spray bottle just over half full with distilled water.
2. Add vodka or white vinegar for preservation.
3. Add essential oils.
4. Hold and charge garnet by visualizing your sexual desire peaking. Feel the sensations running through your body. See yourself having a strong sexual desire filled with passionate, loving experiences. Place garnet into the mixture.
5. Seal and shake to mix well. Hold spray and charge it with passionate energy. Recite the following incantation:

> "Sexual desire come to me,
> Passionate behavior engulf me,
> Sexual desire you trigger in me,
> Sexuality uninhibited I shall be."

6. Spray as needed on your pillow and over your bed covers to induce lusty behavior.

DRINKABLE DREAM TEA

Try drinking the following tea before bedtime. It will help activate the third eye, giving you the ability to dream of a soul mate or a new love. The ingredients are used because of their association with love and relaxation and the ability to aid sleep. By blending these ingredients, you will relax your mind and open yourself to receiving divinely guided messages and visions. This tea is best when created during a Full Moon.

* 2 tablespoons dried peppermint
* 1 tablespoon dried catnip
* 1 tablespoon dried damiana
* 1 tablespoon dried skullcap
* 1 tablespoon dried lemon balm
* 1 tablespoon dried chamomile
* 1 tablespoon dried lemon-grass

1. Ground and center yourself.
2. Combine herbal ingredients in bowl.
3. Let your hands hover above herbs. Charge herbs with intent by visualizing your third eye opening. Visualize the images of unconditional love flowing toward you as the herbs blend, empowering each other to achieve deep REM sleep. Recite the following incantation:

> "O, great and loving maiden goddess,
> Lend your energies into this tea
> So that it may reveal one that will be
> The truest of love, perfect for me."

4. Fill a tea ball with herbal tea mixture. Add to boiling water and steep for 2–4 minutes.

5. While drinking tea, visualize and feel the love already heading toward you. See the colors purple and indigo integrating as your third eye opens and prepares to show you your love.

6. Go to bed and concentrate on having sweet dreams of your loved-one-to-be.

7. Drink this tea anytime you wish to dream of your soon-to-be mate. Store herbal tea mixture remainder in an airtight container for up to three months.

SENSUAL MASSAGE OIL AND MASSAGE

When creating massage oils, choose an appropriate carrier oil to blend with your essential oils. There are many base oils, including jojoba, grape-seed, sunflower, and almond oil. All of them work well, so it is up to you to choose the right base for you. Consider your skin type and the oil's scent and viscosity when you select a base. Almond oil tends to be thicker and spreads well, while grape-seed oil is thinner and tends to be absorbed into the skin with ease. You can also try using store-bought lubricants such as Astroglide or K-Y products as an alternative to traditional massage oils.

* 8 tablespoons apricot kernel oil
* 6 capsules vitamin E
* 3 tablespoons aloe vera gel
* 24 drops Egyptian musk oil
* 8 drops patchouli oil

1. Combine all ingredients in a wooden or glass bowl. Mix well with a wooden spoon. Recite the following incantation:

"Friction and fire,
Burning desire,
Pulsing and beating ever higher.
Shakti, Shakti bless for me,
Shiva, Shiva balance the need,
Passion and tantric waiting to be,
Love and spirituality it shall be."

2. Right before using on your partner, warm oil slowly in a double boiler. Be careful not to overheat it, and remove it immediately if it starts to smoke. Should you feel the need to add more essential oil, use a four-to-one ratio between Egyptian musk and patchouli. Both scents are aphrodisiacs, and you don't want to overpower your partner.
3. Put on some beautiful, soothing music.
4. Now that you have created your atmosphere and a beautiful essential oil blend to use as your massage oil, it is time to perform your magic. Use your own hands as a tool for creating sexual energy with your partner.
5. Have your partner lie face down on the bed, using pillows where needed for added comfort and proper alignment of the spine.
6. Warm up the massage oil by rubbing it between your hands to create friction. Apply massage oil liberally on your partner's skin without allowing the oil to pool.
7. Have your partner concentrate on breathing and listening to the music.

8. Beginning at the neck and shoulders, use long fluid motions to rub lengthwise to reduce any tension and stress. Watch your partner's body language to adjust your motions for good pressure and touch.

9. Bring your hands down the spine and back muscles using consistent, fluid motions.

10. Massage the buttocks and thighs. While rubbing the thighs, start to move your hands up and down the inner thigh, occasionally gently brushing against your partner's private areas. This helps build sexual energy.

11. Continually move up and down your partner's legs, moving down to the feet. Massage the feet according to the likes of your partner. Use great care and caution not to tickle the feet; this will disrupt the sexual energy.

12. Take your time and work all over the body. Have your partner turn over. Beginning at the chest, lightly massage the breasts or pectoral muscles, moving in circular motions around the breasts and nipples.

13. Bring your hands down to the waist in long strokes. Try not to rub too lightly here. Continue rubbing the thighs and around the genital area. This beginning should lead you to a wonderful night of enchanted lovemaking.

—✦ *Magical Musings* ✦—

It is not recommended to perform spells while angry or while on any recreational drug or alcohol. This may impair your spell and bring poor results.

Avocado Love Dip

In many ancient societies, avocados were used to promote sexual activity, fertility, and love. In the following dish, additional ingredients accentuate the purpose of the spell. Serve this as an appetizer or light meal.

* 4 ripe avocados, peeled and pitted
* 2 packages guacamole seasoning
* 16 ounces sour cream
* 1 package taco seasoning
* 9" pie plate
* 1 can refried beans or 2 cups cooked ground beef (optional)
* 1 large tomato
* 1 small onion
* 2 cups shredded cheddar cheese
* 1 bag tortilla chips

1. Mash avocado in a medium bowl with guacamole seasoning. Cover and refrigerate for 30 minutes. Discard pits or use them to grow plants.

2. While guacamole chills, mix sour cream with taco seasoning. Cover and chill.

3. Take a 9" pie plate and spread refried beans or ground beef in the bottom if desired.

4. Hold and charge tomato by visualizing love coming into your life. See how the added love fills your heart, making it whole. While chopping tomato, recite the following incantation:

"By the power of tomatoes, ignite the passion within my life."

5. Hold and charge onion by visualizing the dish enhancing sexual desire and promoting stimulating talks and loving glances. See

this coming to full fruition as you add onion to the dish. While chopping onion, recite the following incantation:

"By the power of onions, increase vitality and desire."

6. Remove guacamole and sour cream mixtures from the refrigerator. In the pie plate, layer one part guacamole and one part sour cream until you have used all the ingredients. Visualize the layers as aspects of the love you desire. As you create this dish, you accentuate and magnify these qualities.
7. Sprinkle the top layer with chopped tomatoes and onions. Visualize the success of your goal. Top with shredded cheddar cheese and bake in a 350°F oven until cheese has melted and begins to bubble over the sides, approximately 30 minutes.
8. Feel free to expand on the ingredients in this dip by adding other items to accentuate love, such as olives, jalapeños, and chives. Serve this dish with warmed tortilla chips and see passion unfold. Feed this dish to each other to add more spice to your night.

✦ Magical Musings ✦

Witches commonly imbue their culinary dishes with a little bit of magic. Saying an affirmation and visualizing love flowing into any meal you create will provide the eater with extra energy.

Coriander Chicken Sauté to Heal Rifts

This is one of those dishes that not only has the power to soothe relationships but also has been known to accentuate love and passion. It magnifies healing properties, which give birth to tenderness between two lovers. This tenderness will soothe fears and allow stronger love and passionate feelings to arise. The main herb here, coriander, is the primary magnifier of the love and passion in this dish.

* 1 pound boneless chicken breasts
* 1 cup flour
* 1 teaspoon salt
* 1 teaspoon pepper
* 2 teaspoons ground coriander
* 1 teaspoon dried marjoram
* $\frac{1}{2}$ stick butter
* 3 shallots, diced
* $\frac{1}{2}$ cup dry white wine
* 2 cups chicken broth

1. Pound and trim fat from chicken breasts. Cut chicken breasts into medallion-sized pieces. Visualize the tenderness you desire. Set chicken aside.
2. In a medium bowl, mix flour, salt, and pepper. Lightly coat chicken in flour mixture and set aside.
3. In a small bowl, combine ground coriander and marjoram. Empower and charge these herbs with the following incantation and set aside:

"Empower and awaken
The love in me.
Empower and awaken
Passion to fill me."

4. Grease large sauté pan and add chicken pieces. Cook chicken over medium heat in stages, and do not overlap or overcrowd. Place cooked chicken on a plate. Set aside.
5. Sauté 2 tablespoons butter and diced shallots until clear. Deglaze pan with ½ cup white wine. Add chicken broth and simmer over medium heat for approximately 15 minutes or until sauce thickens.
6. Serve this dish over white rice.

CHERRY AND CHOCOLATE CHEESECAKE DELIGHT FOR NEW LOVE

The purpose of this delightful dessert is to entice and break the sexual tension in all new relationships. This essential recipe combines aphrodisiacs with the smooth texture of a good cheesecake.

* 4 tablespoons butter, melted
* 2 cups crushed Oreo cookies
* 20 ounces cream cheese
* 1 cup sugar
* 3 eggs, slightly beaten
* 1 teaspoon vanilla
* ¼ teaspoon salt
* 1 heaping tablespoon all-purpose flour
* 2 tablespoons whipping cream
* ½ cup mini chocolate chips
* 1 can cherry pie filling

1. Preheat oven to 450°F.
2. Grease sides and bottom of a 9" springform pan.
3. Add melted butter to crushed cookies and mix well. Press cookie mixture into the bottom of the pan.

4. Soften cream cheese in a large bowl with an electric mixer. Beat in sugar. Add eggs one by one, blending well between each addition.
5. Add vanilla, salt, flour, and whipping cream. Beat until mixture is creamy and fluffy.
6. Fold in chocolate chips and pour mixture over crust.
7. Let your hands hover over the cake mixture to charge it with your intent. Recite the following incantation:

> "Cherries and chocolate sweetness divine,
> Break the tension, two hearts combine.
> Unlock the spring, pleasure be mine,
> Two hearts become one, passion entwined."

8. Bake for 10 minutes. Reduce heat to 200°F and continue baking your cheesecake for 38 minutes or until set.
9. Gently use a butter knife to loosen the edge of the cake from the pan. Cool cake completely before removing rim.
10. Place on a platter and spoon on cherry pie filling. Refrigerate until ready to serve.

— ✦ *Magical Musings* ✦ —

Common ingredients in recipes are great for spellwork in and out of the kitchen. For example, salt has protective qualities and sugar will help add sweetness to your spells. If you want to boost prosperity, add coriander, while cumin will help protect your property.

SEXY SPICED WINE

———— * ————

This warming wine is imbued with the intoxicating effects of love and lust. This is the ideal aphrodisiac wine that you and your partner can drink to set the mood. It is also an excellent recipe to use during the winter months to drive away the chill and warm you up, inside and out. Call upon Bacchus, the god of wine, who not only represents the intoxicating power of wine but also is viewed as a promoter of love and peace. For best results, make this on a Full Moon.

* 3 cinnamon sticks
* 2 tablespoons cardamom seeds
* 2 tablespoons rose hips
* 3 tablespoons whole cloves
* Cheesecloth
* Kitchen string
* 1 cup sugar
* 1 bottle red wine

1. Combine cinnamon sticks, cardamom seeds, rose hips, and cloves in a dry cheesecloth. Tie closed with kitchen string.
2. Dissolve sugar in a medium saucepan with red wine, stirring occasionally.
3. Add spice bundle and allow to simmer on low to medium heat, stirring occasionally, for approximately 20 minutes.
4. While stirring in a clockwise motion, infuse your drinkable potion with the following incantation:

"Bacchus, Bacchus, bless for me,
Infuse my potion, three by three.
Love, passion, and ecstasy,
To share between my love and me."

5. Serve and enjoy.

PASSIONATE CHAI
— * —

This chai drink leaves you feeling alive and sexy. Allow passionate behavior to relieve stress and add excitement to your life.

* ¼ teaspoon licorice pieces
* ¼ teaspoon cardamom seeds
* 1 cinnamon stick, broken up
* ¼ teaspoon black peppercorns
* ¼ teaspoon loose black tea

1. Blend the ingredients.
2. Let your hands hover above the herbs, and charge them with the intention to ignite passion. Visualize red universal energy coming from your hands.
3. Brew to desired strength and enjoy!

— Chapter 5 —

MAGICAL LOVE
IS HERE TO STAY

Now that you know some of the many ways the universe can help you find true love, it's time to think about relationships in a broader sense. Should you ever try to change someone's feelings using witchcraft? How long will you have to wait for the perfect partner? Are soul mates real? This chapter will answer those questions and more as you reframe how you look for love. As a magical being with limitless potential, you can begin to enjoy the process of finding love.

Attracting Others the Magical Way: Do No Harm

You now have learned the tools and techniques that generations of witches before you have utilized to get to know themselves better and to find lasting relationships. Numbers are no longer just math equations waiting to be solved—they hold power and possibility. Your palms contain a story that is greater than you imagined, and the stars spell out probabilities you did not even know existed. The magic that lies within you no longer needs to be dormant—you know how to activate it and manipulate the energies around you. You are a powerful witch!

Before you go search the stars for your next magical match, there are a couple of ground rules to remember when dealing with matters of the heart.

Never Force a Relationship

If you cast a spell for a specific person and that person does not reciprocate the feelings, you must respect their wishes. No matter how hard you try to manipulate the energetic forces of the universe, if you bend someone to your will, you may end up in a relationship that is not at all what you imagined. Forcing another person to be in a relationship with the use of magic usually ends up with unintended consequences for the witch who cast the spell. The relationship may seem great in the beginning, but then the partner may end up cheating and telling lies. You never know what consequences will manifest.

When dealing with matters of the heart, keep things open and vague. Ask for the universe to send you someone with the qualities that will work for you—say, a Leo with a heart of gold and a 5 life path number. This leaves it up to the universe to find the vibratory frequency that complements yours and to bring you that relationship that is destined in the stars.

BE PATIENT

Patience is a skill that wise witches cultivate and practice over many years of work. It may seem frustrating when you have all these tools available to you and you still have not met the partner of your dreams. But, the universe really does work in mysterious ways, and sometimes the timing doesn't match your expectations.

One reason witches have such a difficult time with patience is because when we are dealing with the spiritual realm, we are able to manifest instantly. You may have experienced this in your dream life, where you think of something and it appears. But, when we are living our human life, we have to take time into consideration. Time is a dimension and factor of this world we live in, and sometimes it is frustrating to work with.

That perfect person for you may not manifest in front of your eyes in a day or a week, but, if it is meant to happen, it will happen. The work of witches operates best when they leave it to the universe to decide on timing. Perhaps that individual is not meant to come into your life until you get the promotion that will give you more time and money to spend with them. Or maybe that person who is destined to be with you needs to get out of their current relationship before they find you. If it is meant to be, the universe will allow it to occur.

It's Okay to Be Alone

Another fact of the universe that every witch should know is that not everyone wants to find a perfect match. Not every person here on this planet chose a life path for themselves that involves stable relationships or long-lasting commitments. Some people are perfectly happy living out life single and alone. The relationship you have with yourself is the most important one of all!

When people pair up and form relationships, karma is usually formed. Sometimes people enter relationships to work on karma that they developed from past lives. Sometimes they form new karma. And, sometimes, people living in the world today don't want the burden and responsibilities that come with that karma, so they do not form partnerships.

There is nothing wrong with deciding not to pair up and instead just having casual encounters when you desire—or taking care of yourself. Live your truth and create the best life for yourself, however that looks.

Love Truths

Love is a very powerful force in this universe and a topic that many people think about daily or even hourly. The need to pair off and find a soul mate or a partner can sometimes feel like a job in itself. Watching friends and relatives make lasting commitments or finding romance can sometimes send you into a tailspin, wondering where your partner is and what they are up to now. There are some truths about love that you first need to realize before you spend all day wishing you have what your best friend has.

Twin Flames versus Soul Mates

Some people refer to their partner as their twin flame—that person who complements them so perfectly that they were destined to be together before they were born. But, there is a little truth about twin flames that not many people talk about: Twin-flame relationships are not a fun type of relationship to be in.

Twin-flame relationships are actually exceedingly rare. In these situations, it feels as if one soul has been torn apart. One half is always searching and looking for the other half, and when they finally meet—they ignite. But, the two halves of this one soul are opposites. They tend to like different things and solve conflict in opposing manners, and even their physical appearances can be considerably different.

A relationship between twin flames usually looks very volatile until they can find a way to interact and merge in a manner that works for both their personalities. There tends to be a lot of yelling and fighting as emotions are raised and passion is heated. Through it all, however, there is a soul-level bond that keeps these individuals coming back time and again.

It is much more likely that you will run into your soul mate rather than twin flame. And really, you would probably prefer a soul-mate relationship above a twin flame. While twin flames are the act of one soul being split into two and separated on this Earth, a soul-mate relationship is the act of karma and destiny at work.

Soul mates are also planned before you were born. Sometimes you can even find the possibility of a soul mate written in the stars through astrology. These are individuals whom you chose to have a relationship with before you incarnated here on Earth. They could have previous karma that you need to work out, or they could be a person who will help you grow and advance in your spiritual journey.

LOVE IS BLIND

A love truth that is slowly gaining more recognition in our world today is that there is no one right way for love to look. Love can come in all shapes and sizes and is not meant to look one specific way. Love does not choose to form to societal standards but is designed to bring the perfect individual to you, not to cultural norm.

When looking for love, keep an open mind and open heart. Follow what your heart is telling you. As long as love is consensual, then it is beautiful.

Most Important Love of Your Life

The ultimate true love is hiding right in your own chest. It beats every day and asks you to listen: your own heart. The ultimate truth of love is that first you must love yourself. Before you can really commit yourself to another person, you must find it within your heart to love you. If you don't love yourself first, you may inadvertently try to find a partner that loves you so you don't have to. But that partner will never fill that void that only you can fill.

Sometimes what needs to happen before love can be allowed to enter your life is for you to accept yourself in all your glory. Accept how you look, how you act, how you love. Loving yourself creates a vibrational frequency of harmony and peace that will resonate out into the atmosphere and bring you that love you need.

Love you first, and that partner you have been searching for will appear, as if by magic.

INDEX

◆